Agency Growth Machine

Transform Producer Potential
Into Agency Growth & Profit

*"The highest calling of leadership
is to unlock the potential of others."*

--Carly Fiorina--

Randy Schwantz

Contents

Contents

- The Problems We Solve
- Your Next Step

Foreword

In 2011, I was a thirty year old kid from New Jersey with five years of experience as a producer, selling group health insurance. I was asked to take over as Sales Manager, for a team of nine sales people ranging from 28 to 58 years old. Almost all of them were Property & Casualty specialists, which I knew nothing about (and four years later still have lots to learn). One thing I did know, was that I was entrusted with the authority to create a sales team, and more importantly, a true sales culture, for a firm that had been selling insurance policies for close to sixty years. I was empowered to do this in whatever way I thought would be the most effective. I was embarking on a path I had never traveled, and a path for which I did not know the best course of action. I felt empowered and frightened... but mostly frightened. How was I going to get this team to sell more?

Let me tell you about our agency prior to 2011. We were a firm that spoke about the great relationships we had with our clients and our carriers. We highlighted the hundreds of years of experience that our staff had accrued. We boasted of 'special programs' and 'work comp dividends' to win new prospects over. We believed that our honesty and high ethical standards would act as our competitive edge. For 60 years we quoted on a lot of insurance policies; we would never dare to think of asking for a BOR! Does all of this sound familiar? I bet it does, because we sold insurance just like all of our competitors. We called it 'the old fashioned way'. Many people would call it servicing the client.

When I was chosen to be the firm's Sales Manager, our sales numbers were stagnant; we grew at about 3.3% a year. We had three 'stars', which to us meant guys that wrote $50-100k in revenue year after year. Aside from the stars, the rest of the team floundered. We churned through new producers with only one success in five years (that was me), and I assure you I was far from a sales star.

I quickly realized that I needed help; my three partners and I had the burden of the huge loan payments generated from the pending perpetuation taking place. I felt that if we found the right system, we could begin to help new sales people succeed: A system that could grow our sales numbers and build a culture that could be replicated no matter how big or small we were.

We looked at several different sales consultants, both inside and outside of the insurance industry. It was not until one of my partners read *The Wedge* by Randy Schwantz, that we knew we had found something that would meet our needs. I was confident I could follow the sales process outlined by *The Wedge*. What we didn't know until we conducted more research, is that Randy developed a whole system to turn around your sales culture, called *the iWin Agency Growth System*. This system, when followed, would help us create the sales culture that we desperately needed, to be able to maintain our independent agency structure for years to come.

After our engagement began with the *iWin Agency Growth System*, we started the process of changing some of the things we did at the agency. We did a lot of sales training with our producers; we trained them to win, not just quote. We changed our sales meeting format away from the "spreadsheet liars' club meetings" we were accustomed to, to a much more succinct and powerful process called CRISP sales meetings. That opened the door for us to institute minimum account sizes, and establish minimum sales goals that needed to be attained annually.

Unfortunately there were some negative outcomes to these changes. We heard things like, "How can you take accounts from us? We worked hard to get them!" or "You're taking money from my pocket to make the agency more money!" or "I have built strong relationships with these clients, you can't take them from me!" or "How can you expect us to reach these goals?" A portion of our sales staff decided that the new requirements were not for them. In fact, it helped them realize the industry was not for them altogether.

As for the positive outcomes, our changes provided money to invest in extra resources, in people, and in software that could help us quickly implement a proactive strategy with our clients. With these resources in place our sales people had the ability to approach bigger accounts and offer them something they had never previously thought possible. They were no longer going into accounts asking the prospect, "If we save you 10%, is there any reason you wouldn't be willing to move to us?" They no longer had to rely on finding big coverage gaps or a price so cheap that the incumbent broker could not match it. They now had something tangible to sell that could be replicated and the ability to win new business by BOR. We have seen over 50% of the new revenue we are writing come in via BOR!

Setting a minimum account size and eliminating the 'renewal' and service burden of small accounts on our producers freed up their time to find prospects and set more appointments. They now have the time and ability to start targeting larger accounts. Therefore, their average account size has grown and so has their book of business. The other bonus is that those clients now feel important to the agency, as they have someone they can reach immediately when 'emergencies' arise. They actually feel better now about the agency than they did when working with the producer who had 'built such a strong relationship'.

We have also seen incredible by-products of these changes: The general insurance public has become more aware of what we have become. Carriers want to give us contracts and producers want to work for us. We are giving them a chance to be great! We even had an agency pick our group to sell to instead of one of the big Private Equity firms that are currently flooding the market. The Private Equity firm offered more money, but the Agency Principal wanted a sales culture where he felt he could thrive. We paid less and made a significant acquisition because we have implemented the *iWin Agency Growth System*!

The most tangible result to the agency has been the bottom line. Before we got involved with the *iWin Agency Growth System* we averaged 3.3% growth year over year. Now, we are realizing extraordinary growth! My definition of extraordinary growth is 60% organically over the past 4 years. That equates to organic growth of 15% year over year!

You will never hear me say that our accomplishments were easy to achieve. If anything, you will hear me say how hard it was and how hard it still is today. I was chosen to change the sixty year old sales culture of a Property & Casualty firm, and I was a thirty year old Employee Benefits producer with no experience on the P&C side of the industry. I would be lying if I told you I did not have moments where I wanted to quit. When I was told, "You don't understand, you're a benefits guy; it's different" or, "I've been doing this for twenty years."

Foreword

This was the producer's way of saying, stop changing things, kid! They were happy 'doing their best' and being congratulated for their efforts at the end of the year.

I realized as the Sales Manager and an Agency Owner that, had I allowed the status quo to remain, I would not have been fair to myself and the agency. More importantly, I would not have been fair to our sales people. It was apparent to me that I could not continue to send our sales team out to prospects when in reality they had nothing to sell and had no training to win.

It is my obligation as a Sales Manager and Agency Owner to give my sales team something concrete to sell, and create the best opportunity for them to write business. If they fail, then I have failed. If they succeed, then I have also succeeded. For those that do not know me, I do not enjoy the prospect of failure. For us, the best chance for me to fulfill this obligation was through the implementation and utilization of Randy's system; he and his team have put together a simple method that gives agencies the ability to achieve Extraordinary Growth.

Not only has the agency seen Extraordinary Growth, but our producers are obtaining results that they themselves never believed possible. We are helping producers succeed at unparalleled levels. This success means that they have more disposable income for their families. It means they can send

xii

their kids to the college of their choosing. It means they can buy all of life's extras that are so hard to fit into an average budget that exists from average results. Ultimately, it means we are helping them have the financial freedom they dreamed of when they first committed to selling insurance for our agency.

I am proud to say that we are fulfilling our obligation as an agency. We are seeing Extraordinary Growth. We are helping producers find their financial freedom. This is being accomplished by following a process and ignoring the most recent internal objection.

The results are the proof; if you stick to it and ignore the criticism, the process works!

Jon Sharp
Sales Manager and Agency Principal
Hardenbergh Insurance Agency

Preface

Hi, I'm Randy Schwantz.

The Independent Agency System is changing and there are 3 reasons.

1. Agency Owners are getting older fast.
2. Agencies held off hiring new producers during the 2008-2012 timeframe and are struggling to recover.
3. Venture Capital firms fell in love with the insurance business.

The average age of agency shareholders is up 2 years in just the last 5. Younger shareholders have not been added to the ranks of owners fast enough to keep the average age down.

New producer hiring slowed way down during the recession and agencies are struggling to find enough talented people to hire. Many agencies struggle even more to validate their new producers and turn those investments into profits.

Venture Capital money discovered the Independent Agency System and is investing billions in buying out baby boomers. This year alone 400-600 agencies, and maybe more, will be bought and absorbed. And I'm told by a CEO of one of the aggregators that this trend will last for a while. The Venture Capital firms have access to cheap money. They don't just like insurance agencies - they love them for several reasons: They are highly profitable, have a very predictable stream of revenue, low capital expenditure and they feel there are many ways to turn that Potential into Greater Profits.

As a result they will pay high prices, and baby boomer owners, who can see the light at the end of the tunnel, are gladly putting it in their pockets.

Where are you in this equation? Are you a seller or a buyer? There is certainly a lot of money to be made for the visionary/operator that can harness the resources, manpower and systems to exploit what the big money players are doing.

It's my hope, that as you read this book, you'll become encouraged. You'll see that you too can turn Potential into Profit, just like the others who are moving and shaking in that direction.

Preface

Turning Potential into Profit

Look at your producers and think about this:

What would happen if they were more motivated to prospect, sell and grow their personal income instead of content or apathetic?

What would happen if they were more focused on High Value Activities instead of low value activities, like account service work?

What would having Rock-Solid Differentiation do to their confidence, so they could stand out in this crowded marketplace, instead of having a 'me too' feeling about their value proposition?

What if they had skills and confidence to fill their pipelines with the right kind, right size account instead of waiting for referrals to come in the door?

What if they had a great sales technique and could find or create buyer pain with ease, rather than feeling good about getting a chance to quote?

What if they could close the deal and block the incumbent from getting the last look, instead of getting rolled by the incumbent?

Preface

What if they had a process to retain accounts, so they didn't feel like they were wasting excessive time defending the renewal?

What if they were awesome at cross-selling; getting their partner in the door, each and every time, to act on the opportunity and share in that commission, instead of leaving it there for some other agent to feast upon?

There is Potential -- if your producers were more motivated, more focused, better differentiated, had fuller pipelines, were better at selling, better at closing, got easier renewals and did more cross-selling -- what impact would that have on you, your producers and your profit?

Before you say, "Sounds really good, but won't happen here", please, for your own sake, finish reading this book. Then come back here and ponder that question again.

Your future could be a pleasant surprise…

Randy Schwantz

Introduction

When you really simplify a problem, the problem gets easier to solve.

Most agencies have a growth problem. This simply means they don't, collectively, bring in enough new revenue to grow at a fast pace.

Therefore, owners are not increasing the value of their business. And, as a result, they are not increasing their net worth to any significant degree.

One of my mentors said: "The thinking that got you into the problem is not the thinking that will get you out of that problem. You do have to look at it a different way."

This is a 'How To' book and it's based on my 24 years of working with Agency Owners to help them grow their agencies. I've helped make a lot of people rich, and richer.

You know that GROWTH is not for everyone. Being totally candid, only 3 out of 10 agency owners are ready to benefit from a strategy like this: It's only for those who understand commitment.

Introduction

You're reading a book from a guy that didn't have a clue when he got started. He really only had two things going for him. He was from outside the industry, so he wasn't brainwashed or conditioned to believe that things had to be a certain way. And he's remarkably curious about things like this... so he asked a lot of questions that most people would be embarrassed to ask.

First Discovery

The first big discovery was that most producers in the insurance industry were trained to sell price and coverage. They would set an appointment with a prospect and seek to build a relationship. They would ask some basic, probing questions -- then ask for the policies to compare.

Then they would close the conversation, with something like this: "If I can improve your coverage and save you money, is there any reason why you wouldn't be willing to make a change?" And the prospect would say, "We're open-minded, let's see what you've got."

And with that, the producer would go to work. Six to nine weeks later, they'd be back presenting their proposal. The producer would close with, "Well, can we do business?" And the buyer would say, "I like what you showed me today. Give me a couple of days to review it and let's talk on Friday."

Then, inevitably, the incumbent agent would find out they had competition, find out what the numbers being quoted were, then ultimately find a way to match the competing numbers and keep the business.

A lot of people over the years have called this process, 'getting rolled'. And it was the bane of every producer's existence. It took a couple of years, and a lot of help to figure out a way to reduce that problem and it's called *The Wedge*.

The Wedge

The Wedge is pretty simple.

It just recognizes that there is an incumbent agent. It simplifies the problem for producers and changes their focus during a sales call. Once a producer recognizes there is an incumbent, and that the incumbent has to get fired for them to get hired, it simplifies the problem; it's the incumbent.

Before that, their problem was getting a better price and more coverage from the underwriter. Now their problem is getting the incumbent fired. Hmmm, how do you do that?

Well, it didn't take too long to figure this out.

If you're a producer and you've been a victim of the price and coverage game, if you want to win, you'd better change the game. So there's a way to change the game from price and coverage to a game of service: Not the reactive service that everyone else was doing, but 'Proactive' service that few were doing.

It became really simple. It's the Proactive Service that you do, that the incumbent agent isn't doing... that's where your prospect has pain, but doesn't even know it.

When you can define your list of Proactive Services, your ability to lead a prospect to discover that their agent, the incumbent, is not taking proper care of them becomes relatively easy.

I wrote *The Wedge - How to Stop Selling and Start Winning* in 1998 to document the steps to the process of getting the competition fired (without saying anything bad about them). It was more than 17 years ago, and it still sells like hotcakes, simply because it solves a real problem for insurance agents, and has made a lot of producers and agency owners really well off in the process.

The Inside Story

Truthfully, the early years of teaching and training producers in *The Wedge* were brutal. It went against the grain for a lot of guys, who had been in the business for 10, 20 or 30 years. Many producers felt as though someone was challenging their religion. The pushback by the average producer was enormous.

They had been so brainwashed, that it was all about relationship and their knowledge of coverage. It was about being respectful and having a good reputation. It was about their carrier relationships.

What they didn't know, and wouldn't easily accept, is that everything they said that separated them from their competitors made them look like identical twins. They were a commodity. Their product was a commodity. And their results were mediocre at best.

The typical closing ratio in an agency back then was in the 20-30% range. For most of the producers that have adopted *The Wedge* selling process, the closing rate is in the upper 50% range and many consistently approach 80% -- and most by Agent of Record.

The Cause

Have you ever felt like you were pushing a rope up a hill? If so, you know how hard it is.

Most of the producers weren't very motivated. They didn't like to prospect. They didn't have large books of business. They wouldn't participate in sales meetings.

Introduction

In one-on-one meetings they were asked, "How did you become a producer?"

You might not be surprised, but the path to becoming a producer for a long, long time was to take a trip through a large national carrier.

Now, think about that... what are they going to teach there? A new employee will learn a lot about coverage in the first 24 months, while working in the underwriting department. Then off to the field for 24 months calling on agencies, where they'll learn all about building relationships.

The next step on the career path is to get hired by an independent agency that needs someone who is smart and understands the insurance business; meaning the agency doesn't have to train them in the technical stuff.

Now, if that was your path, and you're a great producer... Congratulations! You made it to the Promised Land. But, a lot of people from that path became really good account managers, working in an agency environment and pretending to be producers. They had been set up to fail, or at best to be mediocre as producers, mostly because they don't like to prospect: Agencies were full of these wonderful people.

They understood coverage and could retain a book, if given to them. They were decent at rounding out an account. But the big problem was that they had no ambition, didn't like to prospect, but were happy to be on the team.

The Next Epiphany

A client in Fort Worth, Texas was in a huge growth mode. They wanted to hire producers, as they were on the growth bandwagon. Every couple of months a new producer would be introduced at the sales meetings. About 1 in 4 seemed pretty sharp, but the other 3 were questionable.

While having lunch with the CEO, I asked him, "Where are you getting these guys?" He told me some came from carriers, some were the children of clients and some were just friends and family.

I then asked him: "You wouldn't mind if I got involved in the hiring process would you?" He said, "Sure, go ahead."

That was in 1995. Ten years later, 34 new producers had been hired, of which 29 had validated and a few had already become Million Dollar Producers. Add it all up, and this group of producers had an aggregate book of business a little greater than 19 million dollars. They averaged $672,000 each.

The epiphany was pretty simple. I had discovered and refined a way to determine, up-front, with a high degree of accuracy, if a producer would and could make it. It worked 29 out of 34 attempts; that's pretty good.

If agency owners are willing to implement what had been learned here, they'll make good hires, not bad ones. If they repeat that cycle over and over, they will transform their agency.

One More Thing

There was an agency here in the Dallas area that had been gobbled up by a well-capitalized firm. Doug, the COO, wanted to find a way to develop a Sales Culture throughout his firm of 7 offices and asked for some advice.

We jointly mapped out a Sales Culture diagram that started at the top of the food chain with the CEO and worked all the way down through sales leaders and producers.

He already knew it, and so do you, that sales training is a waste of money, unless you and the other executives are in the game, supporting it in a significant way.

Before meeting Doug, we were just trainers, and we'd go train all the producers in our system. Here is a typical conversation with a CEO after doing Wedge training with his producers.

Introduction

Mr. CEO, how have things gone since we trained your producers? "Well Randy, a couple of our producers have really latched on to your training." So I'd ask, "What about all the other producers?" And, the CEO would always say, "Well Randy, you know… change is hard for those guys."

At that point, there was no answer to the problem of how to get buy-in from producers, how to turn it into a cultural phenomenon. But, there were plenty of ideas; just hadn't found the brave CEO that was willing to give it a shot.

So, with Doug's help the map got created, and he knew he had to sell his CEO on it and get his involvement for it to be successful. The plan included training and development for all the managers that ran offices in the 5-state region. The last piece of the plan included significant upfront and ongoing training for all of the producers, big and small, old and new; no one was left out.

When all was said and done, Doug had a plan to change his culture.

Fortunately, he liked the plan. He sold it to his CEO, and contracted us to do the work. We had a lot of skin in the game too. If it worked, there would be a big bonus as a reward. If it didn't work, there would be a lot of time wasted, considering all the work we had to put into it.

Twelve months later, Doug put together a report, dated February 20, 2001. In summary it said:

- New Business is up 94%
- The Wedge Returned 20:1 on Our Investment
- The Wedge Helped Develop the Summit Global Partners Sales Culture

That is when the light came on for me. STOP doing sales training and **only** work with people who seriously want to develop their Sales Culture.

The Purpose of This Book is to Help You Develop a Sales Culture and GROW Your Agency (Turn Producer Potential into Agency Growth)

Life is full of lessons, if you're fortunate enough to see them.

Here are 3 Big Discoveries that popped out at us and couldn't be denied.

- Someone has to lose for you to win: If you can't get the incumbent fired, you can't get hired.
- There is a way to determine if a producer will make it before you hire them. You can't rely on traditional hiring methods: It takes an evidence-based interview system.

Introduction

- Sales training is a waste of money. To grow an agency, you must create a **Sales Culture**. It starts at the top and trickles down. There's no other way.

Is it true that only 3 out of 10 Agency Owners have what it takes to pull this off? Rather than debate that, the bigger question is: Do you have what it takes to pull this off? If so, I'll show you how to create an **Agency Growth Machine.**

And, when you operate it as it's been designed to operate, you will get results that are astounding.

The results are heavily documented, so this is beyond theory. It's a proven method that works for those willing to DO what is required, in order for the machine to crank out the right results: Extraordinary Growth.

Chapter 1

Three Universal Challenges Every Agency Owner Must Overcome to Grow Their Agency

Growing an Agency would be child's play, if all your producers were hitting on all cylinders. And it would be a piece of cake, if it was easy to find and hire new producers that could sell.

If that were the case, you wouldn't have to invest much of your time, energy or effort to motivate, coach and drive results.

But it's not that way for most Agency Owners.

There are 3 Challenges that Universally affect agency owners and have a huge impact on their wealth and happiness.

1. The Challenge of keeping the Bottom 80% of Producers motivated and focused on writing New Business and Growing their books.

2. The Challenge of finding and hiring New Producers, who will Prospect -- and can Sell – and, ultimately, become Big producers in the agency.

3. The Challenge of the Agency Owner's Time. After managing the agency and renewing your own book, there is precious little time for you to coach and develop your producers. And so they languish.

In this book, you'll experience the solutions to each of these problems. They have been proven to be successful by 100s of agencies; both large and small.

These are solutions that have helped, literally, hundreds of agencies rapidly move from low or no growth, to high-performing agencies, over a 3-year period of time.

These processes all started as ideas; then they were put into action and tested. Some were thrown out because they didn't work. The ideas that got results were kept and refined over time.

Before we get into the problem/solution phase of this book, let's talk about why this is important.

Chapter 1 – Three Universal Challenges Every Agency Owner Must Overcome to Grow Their Agency

Your #1 Asset

Is it true for you that your #1 income-producing asset, your #1 wealth builder, is your agency?

If so, the math becomes remarkably simple. If you can grow your agency by just ONE Million dollars, you just created $200,000 of annual renewable profit to spend or invest on whatever you choose.

When you can grow your agency by ONE Million dollars, you have just increased the value of your agency and, therefore, your wealth by about $1.5 - $2.5 Million, maybe even more.

The numbers add up fast. For many out there, finding a way to consistently grow your agency is like the search for the Holy Grail. Frankly, it's not that hard, if you have enough discipline to implement a growth system. A growth system is the platform for the financial freedom you want and more of the lifestyle you desire.

The Numbers Are Staggering

We were in a workshop recently, when an Agency Owner held up his iPhone and showed us the news... Biggest independent agency in Dallas, Texas sells out to Marsh. This agency had 76 million in revenue, 350 employees, multiple locations and they sold out to Marsh McLennan Agency, a publicly held company.

Do a search yourself. You'll find publicly owned brokers and big aggregators buying up agencies, like kids raking in candy on Halloween.

I'm told that this year, over 400 M&A deals will be done in North America alone. Some deals are very big, most aren't… but that's a lot of deals.

Feed the BEAST…

Why are these independent agencies selling to anyone?

Obviously, Wall Street and venture capital firms see the insurance business as an industry loaded with pork. There is a lot of fat. Those people with the money feel they can turn their dollars into some big profits by buying independent agencies, providing some leadership and accountability. They'll pull out their scalpels and scrape off some fat and what is left has enough value to trade on Wall Street at multiples greater than what they bought it for.

Chapter 1 – Three Universal Challenges Every Agency Owner Must Overcome to Grow Their Agency

It's the Perfect Storm in a sense. Part 1 of the storm is that there is a lot of cash sitting on the sidelines looking for a home. Since interest rates are so low, there is no money to be made sitting on the cash, so the mindset is, buy some pork, scrape the fat, position it for resale in 5 years or so, and get richer.

Part 2 of the Perfect Storm is this: Independent agency owners got old in the last 20 years, they didn't build a sustainable structure and they are left with only one choice; sell.

Agency Owners Got Old

There are a lot of agency owners today, who started right out of college, working for an insurance carrier in the 70s as an underwriter, then became a marketing rep.

They jumped that ship and bought into an agency in the 80s and 90s and have ridden that wagon for 30 to 40 years. And now, they've gotten old. They are in their late 50s, early 60s, some in their 70s and they see no way out.

Big money is thrown their way and that's the escape hatch for them to get out of the business with a lot of jingle in their pocket.

Chapter 1 – Three Universal Challenges Every Agency Owner Must Overcome to Grow Their Agency

Win/Win/Lose

The big money wins immediately. They bought at a multiple much lower than they currently trade, so they have an immediate profit.

The Agency Owner wins; he has a new job working for a public company for 3 years or so, but has a big check in his pocket.

And the producers and staff; who knows if they won or lost? That's where most of the pork is, and that is where most of the fat will be removed.

3 Things Will Soon Happen:

1. Commission rates will be lowered; they were probably too high anyway.
2. A minimum account size will be established; should have been done anyway.
3. A minimum growth rate will be enforced on producers; should have been done anyway.

That right there will produce some nice bottom line profit… that the old agency owner could have taken advantage of, but fear and friendships stop him from making those business decisions.

Fear and Friendships

More than anything, the biggest inhibitor to doing this for yourself and changing your agency into a high-performing environment is Fear and Friendships.

Fear that if you make changes, everyone is going to jump ship, starting with your biggest and best producer. Since many of your producers have been with you for 20 years, you feel it's unfair to change the commission agreement - even though everything around you has changed.

So, you are stuck… and when Big Brother buys you out, you can blame the changes on them, rather than you taking responsibility as an agency owner, entrepreneur, visionary and making the changes now, to ensure not only the survival of your agency, but position it to thrive for 20 more years as a new generation takes over.

Big Brother Isn't Through

Big Brother, the new owner, will encourage you to start hiring new producers to refurbish the place, as the older guys retire or die.

That's another thing you 'coulda/shoulda' done, but didn't.

Well, you will now and you will fund it with the profits that were created when they (Big Brother) got the renewal commission rate right, and quit paying out commission on the small rinky-dink accounts that producers were sitting on.

And, the new owner will bring in a new mentality: Grow or Die.

Grow or Die...

They don't really mean that as a corporation we have to grow or die. They are already committed to grow and they will do it.

What they mean is, you need to grow, or you will die. In other words, you won't be here very long if you don't grow this profit center (it used to be your agency).

Chapter 1 – Three Universal Challenges Every Agency Owner Must Overcome to Grow Their Agency

The Ear of an Agency Owner

As an Agency Owner, I know you have a lot of people in your ear every day trying to convince you to do something.

Your commercial lines manager is telling you, "We need more staff, we need a software upgrade".

Your top producer is reminding you how important he is, and that he is such a good salesperson that he could have done it anywhere. So don't change anything, or he's not sure he'll be around.

You have producers; they are sitting on their books, not writing any new business, they don't prospect... they really don't contribute anything. But they do remind you of the good times, back in the old days, when you guys grew up together. It's just a gentle reminder that we are friends, and they want you to remember that if you decide to make any changes around here... "Since we are friends, you don't mind excluding us from that requirement, do you?"

It's enough chatter and static to drive you crazy. And if you're not really on your game, you will postpone making some really important decisions that will affect the future of your agency in a very negative way.

Chapter 1 – Three Universal Challenges Every Agency Owner Must Overcome to Grow Their Agency

Potential into Profit

The bottom line is this: There is probably a lot of POTENTIAL embedded in your agency. It's like an oil deposit out in the middle of the desert. To turn that Potential into Profit, you're going to have to drill for it. It will not rise to the surface on its own.

And what you'll learn right now is how to start that process, and sustain it long enough to where it becomes a habit; a way of doing things. Once you do, you'll never look back.

Chapter 2

How to Motivate the Bottom 80% (Challenge #1)

The Top 20% of your producers are great sales people. You're probably one of them. You guys produce year in and year out. You hit your numbers and, in fact, you are probably carrying the agency on your shoulders. If not for you, your agency's growth would be flat or maybe even going backwards a little.

The Bottom 20% of Your Producers

Then there is the Bottom 20% of your producers. Some of them are new, so they get a one year reprieve. But, the other ones are probably misclassified. They aren't producers, have never been producers – and they shouldn't even be in that role.

The problem is no one had the guts to tell them that they'd be a lot happier doing something else. (And you'd be happier if you relieved them of their job.)

The pressure of prospecting is just too much for these people. They don't have the drive of a successful producer: They are scared people, albeit with big friendly smiles.

Do them a favor and put them on a plan that causes them to either grow or quit. Make the details and criteria in your plan so black and white, that there is no way to misunderstand what it takes for them to keep their job as a producer.

But be fair, by all means. Give them a reasonable amount of time. And train them, teach them and help them with their prospecting and selling skills.

You have to keep in mind that relieving them of their job is not punitive. But it could be seen that way by your staff and other producers, if you don't invest both time and money in supporting them and helping them. If you don't, this could ruin the goodwill you've built with your support staff, as well as some of the other producers.

Ultimately it is good business and everyone knows it. In fact, you also lose goodwill and destroy the culture of your agency when you let any non-performer stick around -- be it a producer or someone on your support staff.

And, most importantly; if they hit their numbers, congratulate them (and yourself). But let them know this is not a one-time thing. It's your new way of doing business.

If they don't hit their numbers, you must stick to your guns and professionally show them the door. As they walk out, give them a hug and wish them the best. You might even throw them a party. Seriously, you've saved them from a lifetime of struggle because they were simply not suited for insurance sales.

All we've talked about so far is cleaning up your mistakes; the bottom 20% of your producers that are in the wrong job. Now, let's talk about the GOLD -- the middle 60% of Your Producers.

The Middle 60% of Your Producers is A Gold Mine

Your GOLD is buried in the Middle 60% of your producers. And, whether you are mining for gold or drilling for oil, you have to go deep to get it. That's why it takes a disciplined approach. There's just no other way.

You can squeeze a few more shekels out of your top 20 percenters, if you instill a sales culture development process.

And, with the bottom 20%, you MUST clean up your mistakes. Get them up to speed, happily producing, or out. Stop tolerating habitual failure. No good can come of this -- Ever.

But it's with the middle 60% of your producers where you can have a huge impact on their lives and financial independence and consequently, your own growth and profits.

Let's look at this group, the middle 60%, objectively. They are neither your best nor are they your worst. They have to be reasonably smart to have gotten this far. They have to be somewhat driven, or they'd be at the bottom.

They are more than capable of playing the insurance selling game at a much higher level, aren't they?

There is POTENTIAL here and YOU CAN turn it into Profit for your producer and your agency, but you need a system to do it.

If you look at your producers as a problem, your thinking will never lead you in the direction you want.

Think instead, How Do I Turn This Potential into Profit? It's not a Producer Problem…

It's a Leadership Problem

How many times have you heard about a situation where a new Coach takes over a high school or college team and the team starts winning? The only thing that's changed is the Coach.

Some of these Coaches are a Player's Coach, meaning, they build great relationships with their team, getting to know them personally. They find out what's important to their players and help them obtain their goals. And, as a result, their players put out more, practice harder, play harder. Bottom line result…They win more games.

Then you have the Systems Coach. Tom Landry of the Dallas Cowboys was a Systems Coach. Cold, impersonal -- he believed in his system. He believed that if you ran his system, you'd be successful. So he found players that would run his system.

It may not matter whether you're a Player's Coach or Systems Coach, but your players need a coach that can Turn Their

Potential into Revenue, and that's why YOU or SOMEONE in your firm MUST be a Coach.

How many times have you seen a self-organized team beat a well-coached team?

It could happen, but it would be rare; unless the self-organized team has <u>unbelievable</u> talent. That is why you MUST become a Coach -- and drive their efforts, their skills, and their intent to win and grow.

If you don't become a good Coach, you have a self-directed team that you HOPE will grow. But hope is not a strategy, is it?

So, why are your middle 60% producers not writing more new business, attacking larger accounts and growing faster?

The Middle 60% Never Intended To Grow

The first and biggest problem that the middle 60% of your producers have; they never intended to grow big books and make a lot of money.

Let me repeat that. They are not writing more new business or bigger accounts and are not making more money... because they never intended to.

How do you know they never intended to?

It's pretty simple when you really think about it. Ask them to get out their goal setting notes, their journal, their spreadsheet or whatever they use to doodle, think, plan and dream. Chances are you won't see it, because they don't have it.

For the most part, they don't have goals beyond whatever you are asking them to provide you on an annual basis. So they have no reason to bust their hump and go conquer the world. It was never instilled in them as a child, and in most cases it's not being creatively developed in them as an adult.

To generalize, most of them are pretty happy with themselves. They probably make more money than they ever thought they would. They make more money than their parents, their siblings, and most of their friends make. And they are patting themselves on the back, feeling really successful, in relationship to their point of reference.

They are comparing themselves to those who have done less than them, not to their POTENTIAL, their undeveloped capability. Instead, their point of reference could, and perhaps should, be what it's going to take to have a bold and beautiful, financially independent future. But it's not, because no one ever helped them take the time to write down their goals to achieve their dreams… their parents didn't, and chances are it's not a process you drive in your agency either.

As the leader, YOU COULD do this. And it's not that hard. In fact, I'll show you how over and over in this book. As you do these things, you are turning on the Growth Activators; you are Turning Potential into Profit.

Napoleon Hill had a quote:

**"Every adversity has the seed
of an equivalent or greater benefit."**

If you have producers, you have problems. In those problems is an opportunity to Turn Potential into Profit.

If you will accept and take responsibility for all of those problems, you will be in control of fixing them.

If, however, you blame your producers, the industry, the software companies, your support staff – or maybe even your spouse -- for where your agency is right now... you're playing the victim role. And victims are always at the mercy of others.

Choose to be the Victor, Never the Victim.

So look at your situation realistically. Accept the fact that if you want things to change, if you want things to be better, you have to accept that everything that's not working in your agency... is a LEADERSHIP PROBLEM.

When you look at things this way, it creates FREEDOM to change what is not working.

If you don't look at it this way, you will probably be miserable.

In simple terms, until you accept responsibility, you can't fix it.

If your producers are not MOTIVATED, whose responsibility is it?

Of course, it's your responsibility; to help them think about their goals, their future, their family and their retirement fund. And write down a plan of HOW to get them there.

During our training sessions, over 2,500 producers have been asked, "What is your new business goal for the year?" You'd be amazed how many of them have $50,000 as a new business commission goal.

Then they were asked "How did you come up with that goal"?

Here is the part that will blow you away; most of them made it up on the spot. They only set goals to get you, the leader, off their backs. What's worse; there is no correlation between their annual new business goal and what they want for their life.

Let's get more specific…

If you have a producer, who has a family, maybe with as many as 3 kids; they have a huge financial burden that most of them are only vaguely aware of.

With 3 kids, they will have to buy 3 cars. They will have to fund 3 college educations. They'll also have to pay for 1 to 2 weddings, if they have a daughter or two. And, they will have to fund their ability to live beyond the job, through retirement.

Do you think your producers have honestly thought about the CORRELATION between their ANNUAL NEW BUSINESS COMMISSION GOAL and their ability to fund those obligations?

How Much Money do Producers Need?

This is a really important question.

Ask your 35-40 year old, middle 60% producer with a couple of children this question: "Do you know how much money you need to have in your retirement account, so you can live happily ever after when you decide to quit working?"

They'll say something like, "Sort of… well I think so."

Press them on that question, and they'll finally tell you, they don't know.

Then ask them, "How much money do you need to save every year, between now and then, to be able to have that much money at retirement?"

"I'm not exactly sure," they'll reply, if they're being honest with you.

"OK, so in order to save that much money, how big does your book of business have to be, do you know?"

"No, I don't."

"OK then, how much new business do you have to write, to grow your book, to be able to save that much money every year, so you'll have the future you want? Do you know?"

"No, I guess I really don't."

They Don't Know. They Don't Know. They Don't Know.

Isn't it clear, that if you don't have motivated producers, you'll never grow your agency?

Isn't it clear, that sustainable motivation comes from within the producer?

You may be tempted to say: "That's up to them, and I can't influence it." But, things couldn't be further from the truth. You influence it, by doing goal setting that integrates the future with the now. It's your job to help bring their 'intrinsic motivation' into crystal clear focus.

Intrinsic Motivation is behavior driven by internal rewards. In other words, the motivation to engage in a behavior arises from within the individual, because it is intrinsically rewarding.

How many of your producers talk about their kids? Do you enjoy talking about yours? Aren't you proud of their successes? Don't you enjoy talking about the game last night and how your kid played?

You know, without thinking about it very much, that the #1 most important thing to a lot of your producers is their family; specifically their kids.

You hear parents talk about where their kids will be going to college, how much the tuition is and how important a great education can be.

Here is the point. If you want to tap into your producers' INTRINSIC MOTIVATION, that naturally exists, to want to take care of their family – both now and into the future -- you have to change your annual goal setting process into a life goals process.

Discover a New Reality

Most producers do not know, that they have to save somewhere in the range of $55,000 to $65,000 a year for over 20 years to build the nest egg they really want, in order to live successfully into the future... and throughout retirement.

If they did know, and you could help them engineer a plan to write new business, grow their books, earn more money, save more money... and create a great future for themselves and their kids... what would that do to their motivation?

If your producers are not very bright, if they don't care about their family, if they have ZERO confidence in themselves, this might not have an impact.

Or, if they were born with a trust fund, then this might not have an impact.

But if they do have a heart, if they do have a brain, if they do have children, and if they plan to live beyond the day they retire -- this could be highly effective in changing their motivation today, and for years to come, about how they prospect and sell.

Chapter 2 – How to Motivate the Bottom 80% (Challenge #1)

Review

You want to grow your agency.

To grow your agency you need motivated producers.

For the average person to be motivated, they have to be in a motivating environment. That's extrinsic motivation. The outside forces cause them to think about what they want.

The outside forces create a fun, competitive environment. The outside forces set up rules; do this and you write new business, do this and you get rewarded, do this and you keep your job. That is all extrinsic motivation and it comes from having a great Sales Culture. That's one thing you can do to create a lot of external motivation for producers.

But there is also intrinsic motivation, and it comes from the inside. And for you to help them tap into the inside motivation, you have to bring into clear focus -- all of the things that are personally important to them -- and cause them to think about it in the context of:

"How much money will I have to make and save to take care of those most important to me?"

If you have a bunch of hippie producers working for you; living in the moment, possibly divorced several times and they wear Birkenstock's, Tommy Bahama shirts and belong to the local cannabis club -- then you might be screwed. You don't have producers; you have a commune.

But, if you're fortunate enough to have mature human beings, good family people and intelligent insurance professionals, then you have reason to hope.

Your biggest challenge now is helping them to **vividly** comprehend that THEIR FUTURE IS BEING CREATED TODAY. And that future is in direct proportion to their savings ability over the next 20-year period. (Older producers will have to work and save even more.)

Creating Perspective

Have you ever had a kid struggle with a class in high school, maybe a 16-year old, struggling with Math class? They tell you: "I want to be a radio broadcaster, and Math has nothing to do with broadcasting. So, why do I have to take this stupid Math class?"

You Have To Get Them Connected to Two Things…

So you tell your child: "**First,** if you don't make good grades, you won't have to worry about being a radio broadcaster, unless you plan on doing a show on the internet for free".

You know the story; good grades get you into a good college. And a good college opens the door to a good job. A good job is being a radio broadcaster and being able to make a living.

Second, you have to help them see that being a radio broadcaster has a lot to do with Math. You know… counting minutes in a show… how much for commercial, how much casual chatter and how much for real content. That's all Math.

Here's the point: You help your child connect the dots on why making good grades now will make a big difference in their future.

The same is true with your highly intelligent, sophisticated insurance professional, who thinks prospecting, selling, growing their book, making more money, saving more money and preparing for the future is stupid.

It's only stupid, if they think Social Security, Medicare and Medicaid are good options for retirement.

It's only stupid, if they want their kids to go to a community college or take out college loans.

It's only stupid, if they want their kids to drive a rent-a-wreck when they turn 16.

And it's only stupid, if they want to put their daughter's wedding expenses on their American Express card and pay 18% interest on it for the next 12 months, while struggling to pay it off.

Enough on Producer Motivation… On to the Next Issue:

Time

The middle 60% of your producers have a second problem that needs to be addressed. They have way too many small accounts that they can hide behind. They're busy alright; just busy on the wrong stuff.

Being really busy, taking care of small clients and renewing small accounts, is a great reason to postpone prospecting and selling.

Working on too many small accounts ties producers to their desks, instead of out prospecting… and WINNING bigger accounts.

One might think it admirable, even noble, that the middle 60% of your producers would sacrifice their future, their income, their pride, their children, their free time… and even the growth of your agency to take care of the small businesses in the world.

> *"Ladies and Gentlemen, get on your feet and put your hands together… look at these sacrificial people, look at what they have done for the small businesses in America. They have sacrificed their own ambitions to sit at their desk, day in and day out, and answer mundane insurance questions, assist in getting out certificates, adding automobiles and routing endorsements - when they could have been out selling, increasing their own personal income. These people understand personal sacrifice; they are special."*

Being busy is not the same as being productive. Statistics abound. And you, no doubt, have your own. Here are the results of an eye-opening research project. Neither the agency principals nor the producers realized this until it was published in black and white.

Pareto Lives: The 80/20 Rule…

Here are the results of a research project which included 17,808 commercial accounts, 168 producers and $92 million in revenue.

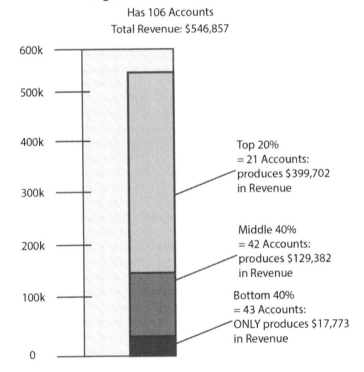

Average Producer's Book of Business

Has 106 Accounts
Total Revenue: $546,857

Top 20%
= 21 Accounts:
produces $399,702
in Revenue

Middle 40%
= 42 Accounts:
produces $129,382
in Revenue

Bottom 40%
= 43 Accounts:
ONLY produces $17,773
in Revenue

Here is the AVERAGE Summary for 168 Producers; the average producer has:
- 106 commercial accounts and $546,857 in revenue
- Average revenue per account is $5,159

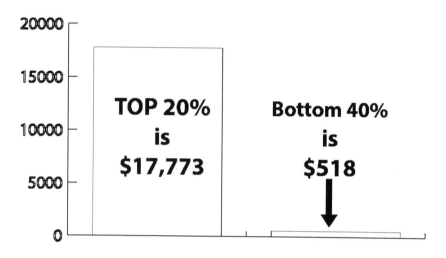

The top 20% of their accounts, bring in $399,702

The average revenue per account for the top 20% of their accounts is $17,773

The bottom 40% of their accounts, of which there are 43, bring in $22,303

The Average Revenue per account for the Bottom 40% is $518

Here is the Insight

43 accounts bring in $22,303 for an average of $518 revenue per account. It's less than 4.1% of the revenue, but 40% of the accounts.

If a producer would write 1.25 more of their top 20% accounts, they could say goodbye, and never miss, the 43 small, time-consuming, low revenue generating accounts that bury them and their support staff in non-productive activities.

Just think about it; if a producer wrote only 1.25 more of their Large Accounts, they could say goodbye to 43 small accounts. It's about a 40:1 tradeoff.

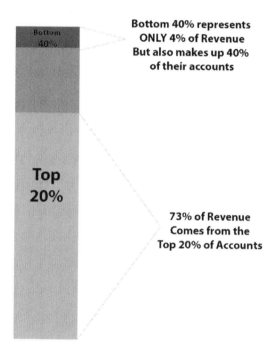

**Percentage of Revenue:
Top 20% vs. Bottom 40%**

Bottom 40% represents
ONLY 4% of Revenue
But also makes up 40%
of their accounts

Bottom 40%

Top 20%

73% of Revenue
Comes from the
Top 20% of Accounts

Do the math: 73% of a producer's revenue comes from 20% of their accounts, and only 4% of their revenue comes from 40% of their accounts.

The logic here dictates, that if you are a producer and you could get rid of 40% of your renewals, 40% of your service calls, and 40% of the burden on your support staff, in exchange for writing a little more than ONE account, you'd want to do it to free up time and make the static go away.

Bring In The Agency Growth Doctor...

If you were an Agency Growth Doctor, what REMEDY would you prescribe for your producers to help them grow?

Would you say to add more of the small, low revenue, time-consuming accounts that cause you and your support staff a lot of work and bring in almost no money?

Or would you say to get rid of the small stuff, get it out of your books – then coach, lead, drive them to write more of those TOP 20% accounts?

Here is a fact; they've already proven they know how to write bigger accounts, because they're in their books. The only reason any self-respecting, intelligent, professional insurance agent would push back on this plan, is because of a lack of confidence and no real goals to grow their income in a significant way.

As the professor said: "It's not rocket science."

What Happens to the Small Accounts?

What do you do with all of those small accounts?

Here are 3 things you can do:
1. You can sell them to someone who wants them.
2. You can send them to the service center of your favorite carrier.
3. Or, if your firm is big enough, you can set up a small accounts department -- give the department a professional name, so your producers can feel good about sending small accounts over to it.

When you do this, two great things will happen for your agency.

The first is this; you will help free up time for your producers, so they can prospect, sell and retain more of the larger accounts. That will enable them to grow their books and by growing their books they make more money. Guess what? You'd make more money too. That sounds like a WIN/WIN.

Secondly, these smaller accounts will have a better home where they are appreciated, taken care of and serviced better. That's a WIN/WIN/WIN; good for the account, good for the producer and good for your agency.

If your producers still want to write small accounts, pay them the first year's commission on it and that's it. When you do this, you'll solve the TIME problem, which leads to solving the real problem... Agency Growth.

Solving the Real Problem... Agency Growth

Problem number one was **MOTIVATION**. Hopefully you are in agreement; if your producers aren't motivated from the inside out and the outside in, they won't produce. If they don't produce, your agency won't grow. If your agency doesn't grow, the American Dream just died.

You might be thinking about using the goal setting process as a technique or tactic to motivate your producers. That would be a mistake. It's not a tactic, it's a strategy.

All I mean by that is this... You need to build a culture around helping your producers double their personal income. It's a strategy. That means you will not just do it once, you'll make it a part of the strategy. You will find additional ways to get them to think about their future, connect it with the present... and do it over and over and over.

Some of your producers will hear the 'double your personal income strategy' and it will have an immediate impact on their behavior, meaning they will start working harder almost immediately.

Others are kind of thick 'upstairs', some of them don't really trust your intentions and some are just obstinate.

That's why you have to, strategically, do it over and over, and over. It will take some of them several years to get it. That's unfortunate, but a reality. If you start it, then stop, it will look like manipulation and you sabotaged your own success.

The other reason to do it over and over and over is the same reason you run sales meetings over and over and over. It just makes sense if you want to drive results.

It's Not Time Management, It's Time Utilization

All millionaires, multi-millionaires, and billionaires – have the same 24 hours a day allotted to them.

It's not how much time you have; it's how you use it. At least that much is clear, right?

If your producers aren't using their time to prospect and sell new accounts, bringing in new revenue on a very predictable basis, then they are either too deep in the weeds servicing their accounts, (doing the CSR's job), or they are spending too much time on the golf course.

If you want to grow your agency and do what's in the best interest of your producers, get them doing the Top 5 Money-Making Activities of Million Dollar Producers.

Top 5 Money Making Activities of Million Dollar Producers:

1. Written Service Timeline

Hire a Marketing Research firm to go to the top accounts in your agency and get them to ask this: *"What is your agent going to do for you over the next 12-24-36 months?"*

What would they say?

Would they say something like this, *"Well, we really like our agency: They're good people. If we have a problem, we call them and they are good to respond. If we need certificates, they get them delivered. If we have claims, they'll help us get them reported. If we buy a building, they'll get it insured. And they always visit us at least once a year"*.

"They also come out for renewal and update information – and, of course, they never miss the opportunity to come back out and pick up a check. They do a good job."

Or would they say, *"Let me show you this written service timeline we use. It has everything they said they would do, along with when it will happen."*

There are two reasons a written service timeline is important...

First reason: To increase retention. If you can increase your retention rate, by only 1%, that will have a huge impact on growth and profitability. Just 1%!

Second reason: When this timeline is well-defined and mutually agreed to, your client has a much better story to tell when introducing you to people they know, which leads to Money Making Activity #2 on the list...

2. Get Red Hot Introductions

There are few producers worth their salt that don't believe they have great client relationships. However, there are few producers who, with any frequency, actively ask their clients to introduce them to people they know.

And there is a reason for that. They're afraid.

What are they afraid of? They don't want to impose on their clients. What does that mean? It means, they don't really feel, or believe, they deserve the introduction.

Producers will use the excuse that they forgot or were too busy to ask, but the truth is, they are either really afraid or just don't care. What else would make sense to intelligent, competent, educated and professional sales people? Nothing!

The ONLY way to deal with fear is to acknowledge it.

Courage is taking action in the presence of fear. It's a 2-step process; acknowledge there is fear, then, you must take action. If you try to avoid fear, it will control you.

Apathy could also be the reason someone would never ask for an introduction. This is actually harder to overcome than fear. Those, who don't give a darn and don't want to make more money, unfortunately, are not made of the stuff you need in a producer. For most leaders, it's hard to cut the cord on those that aren't really doing anything wrong, but they aren't doing anything that an account manager doesn't do. They are not a producer, but they are getting paid like it.

Of course the third and fairly logical reason is that the culture of your agency just never drives a process like this, so they have never even thought about it.

So, don't leave it to chance... build that into your goal setting, sales meetings and coaching sessions.

Can you see how a written service timeline will take away a producer's fear? It works, because your producer has just given the client everything he wants from a service perspective. It is documented, it was co-created. It removes the ambiguity that generally pervades most client-producer relationships. Your producer no longer feels like they are imposing; if done right, your producer feels like they deserve the introduction. They are bringing value that this client has never had before.

When the timeline is in place, asking the client for introductions takes on a different tone, doesn't it?

Gone are the days when producers feel a sense of humiliation when asking for an introduction. This approach, when integrated with the written service timeline, changes everything for the goal driven, intelligent and proactive service producer.

Think about this... How many prospects are there that would immediately take the time to see you, if one of your clients made the call and introduced you in? On the other hand, you could cold call those prospects until you are blue in the face, and they won't answer your call, they won't return your call; they have no desire to meet with you.

Getting introduced in is a Really Powerful way to meet new prospects - you already know this. However, to what degree is it happening in your firm? More importantly, how many dollars of revenue are left on the table day after day?

Here is the next step.

3. Prepare to WIN

How many of your competitors are going to roll over and play dead when you come after their business? No one is.

Is it fair to say that this is a fundamental truth, if you sell commercial insurance?

Someone has to lose for you to WIN.

Chapter 2 – How to Motivate the Bottom 80%
(Challenge #1)

The incumbent agent who is on the account now, controls your future money. If you can't get them fired, you can't get hired.

It's a hard truth, but fundamental to your producers' WINNING.

Preparing your producers to win an account is a fundamental part of a great sales meeting. Most sales meetings, however, are akin to a "spreadsheet liars' club" sales meeting.

How are your sales meetings going?

When you get out the spreadsheet and ask a producer: "*So you're working on Exodus Construction, how's it going?*" What does every producer say, "*Oh, pretty good*".
"*Well, tell us about this opportunity*".

"*Ok, I met with them. They are not happy with their service. I have a couple of markets lined up. I'm feeling pretty good with the relationship. If all goes well, we have a pretty good chance.*"

Now, with all respect, what did they just say? Nothing!

So in preparing them to WIN (not just quote) the account, you have to put them on the spot and make them defend to you, and the rest of the sales team, why this account would be better served by them than the incumbent.

In the beginning, they will freak out. They'll wonder why all the pressure. In the long run, as they get better and better at articulating what they do better than the competition… they'll win more business.

As the Agency Owner/Sales Manager, you'll finally have done your job really well: You prepared them to WIN, you built their confidence, and you helped them leverage your investment in differentiated service that your agency provides. You helped them make it less about price and coverage (which is too easy for the incumbent to match) and you made it about differences that will set them apart from the incumbent.

And when they WIN, you WIN. They make more money and your agency grows. It's a WIN/WIN, is it not?

4. Go Sell (WIN)

Most people think they have this figured out. Most folks think that all you have to do is build a trusting relationship with your prospect.

You simply get them to open up and spill the beans about 'all the pain they are feeling with their insurance program'. Do some trial closes to confirm you have a qualified prospect, grab a copy of the policies, loss runs and financials... then go to work.

For the next few months, you work with underwriters and loss control people to get enough interest to get someone to offer you a competitive price.

A few days later, you present your proposal and book the revenue.

The only problem is this: The incumbent is not likely to sit idly by, and watch this account get stolen from him, is he? Of course, all of the great sales training programs turn a blind eye to the incumbent... "Go sell yourself, they say".

If you were the incumbent, what would you do? You'd pull out all the stops and go for every ounce of guilt and loyalty you could. You'd plant seeds of doubt. You'd have your finger on the hotline to your underwriter just in case you need them to make a price adjustment on the account. And if your tactics were successful, as the incumbent, you'd keep the business.

So, first off, that is why the previous step is so important, you must change your sales meetings from a "spreadsheet liars' club" sales meeting to a meeting that really prepares your producers to win. And when prepared, your producer must execute a sales process that incorporates, not only building a relationship with your prospect, but driving a wedge in the relationship between your prospect and the incumbent agent. If you can't get your competition fired, you can't get hired. Otherwise, there is a great chance the incumbent will leverage their relationship, get last look, match your proposal and your producer will get rolled and end up with a sad tale of woe; but not the win.

5. Get Your Partner in to Cross-Sell the Account

How much money are your producers leaving on the table, because there is no well-formed cross-sell strategy in your agency? And, what is the financial impact on your agency's profit and growth? Equally important, what impact does that have ultimately on the retention of accounts?

There are at least two reasons why more accounts are not cross-sold. One is a generally accepted belief in the agency that the producer owns the account. They prospected it, they built the relationship, they wrote it; it's theirs.

Sounds logical, right?

However, this view runs the common risk of closing the door to other producers when someone is a little possessive about 'their' accounts. Understandably, they don't want others to screw up their relationship out of ineptness.

The second challenge is **access** to opportunities. And I know you'll say this is being overstated. Just ask yourself this question; when was the last time a report was printed and distributed, so that all producers could peruse it and find cross-sell opportunities?

When was the last time you put it up on the projector and walked through them one by one, assigning producers to accounts where the P&C is written but the health insurance isn't, or vice versa?

Take this to the extreme, what if your producers had 'instant' access, anywhere, anytime, to survey and capitalize on those opportunities?

Granted, no one needs instant access. You don't need instant access to your bank account on your phone, but you probably have it. You don't NEED instant access to your investment account, but you have it. And you don't need instant access to all your contacts on your mobile device, but you have it. And, now that you have it, you'll probably never go back to the way it was.

Having instant information right at your fingertips is no longer a luxury; it's the way of the 21st century. You want what you want when you want it.

And so would many of your producers, who may want to partner up with other producers to cross-sell an account.

But, if you're like most agencies… it's not like that. Producers have to go through one or two people and wait an ungodly amount of time to get an outdated, incomplete report.

That's too cumbersome. No one has time to wait. And, unless you and your partners create easily-accessible systems that'll spit out information at the speed of a mouse-click, you'll be challenged to experience and drive extraordinary growth from cross-selling.

When you get your producers working in the Top 5 Money Making Activities, they will WIN a lot of new business. They will retain more of their existing accounts. Their books will grow faster. They will be happier. You'll be happier. Your agency will grow and life will be good.

Summary for Challenge #1:

How do you motivate the bottom 80% of your producers to get out of bed every day and go sell insurance – to prospect frequently and WIN new accounts, which will grow their books of business?

The reality is; you probably can't. The Bottom 20% of your producers need help to either get up to speed or get out. Don't be punitive or angry -- just help them find their way to either produce or get another job somewhere.

The Middle 60% of your producers represent your Gold. They are reasonably smart, reasonably driven, but they need direction. You shouldn't expect them to self-manage their way to the next level of progress. They need a leader.

This creates the hardest question of all…

Do You Want To Lead Your Team?

If your answer is "Yes", there is a promise of More Money, More Financial Freedom and More Fun. But it's a journey, not a destination. It's something you have to commit to, not just try.

Is it worth the investment? You know it is.

Are you personally capable of doing it, pulling it off, being relatively consistent? That's the big question that has to be addressed.

I'm sure you're familiar with the great motivational speaker, Zig Ziglar? One of his famous sayings was:

"You can have everything in life you want, if you will just help enough other people get what they want."

Help your producers achieve their goal of doubling their books of business, doubling their personal income and achieving financial independence. This will make the achievement of your goal a natural result.

Chapter 3

How to Hire Great Producers (Challenge #2)

Finding, Hiring and Developing new producers is a time consuming, difficult and expensive endeavor. It's even worse if you're bad at it.

And if you're really good, say in the top 25% of agencies, it will create an amazing amount of shareholder equity (that's code language for wealth).

Does your agency need to hire new producers to stay in the game long term? If so, what are your chances of making a good hire, retaining that producer, having them consistently write new business and then repeating that cycle?

Well, you're about to see some statistics that will probably make you reach for your depression meds, but don't lose hope, there is a bright light shining on the backend of this chapter… if you have the perseverance to get through the darkest part.

Compare Those Who Have and Those Who Have Not...

Just look at the first two columns of the chart on the next page. The 21-40 age group in the average agency controls 15.1% of the total revenue in the agency. In the high growth agency (they hired new producers) that doubles to 30.3%.

Look at it from the other end and here is what it says: In the average agency, the 51-60+ age group control 51.9% of agency revenue. In the high growth agency that is only 38.4%.

Not a problem, money is money... but who will control that money in 5 years and 10 years if the average agency doesn't figure a way to recruit, hire and develop new producers?

**Weighted Average Book of Business
by Age Group**

Average Agencies vs. High Growth Agencies

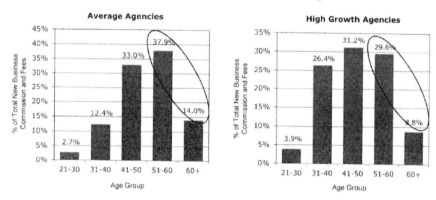

Commission & Fees Controlled by Producers Over 50 years = 51.9% vs. 38.4%

When you look at just new business written, average vs. high growth agencies, you see the same problem.

In the average agency 19.9% of new business is coming from the 21-40 age group. In high growth agencies 40.8% is coming from the 21-40 age group. In average agencies 43.9% is coming from 51-60+ and 38.5% is coming from 51-60+.

Again, you get the picture; just project your agency 5 years and 10 years down the road and what have you got (if you're the average agency)? For the most part, your agency is a candidate to get bought by an aggregator, because you are too far down the road to recover, which means you can't hire enough new talent to keep the agency going. You will have to sell or hold on and grind to a slow finish.

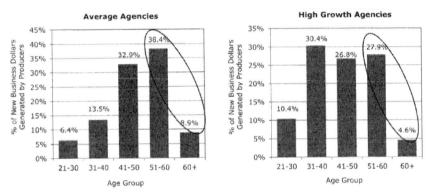

Average Agencies vs. High Growth Agencies

New Business Generated By Producers Over 50 years = 47.3% vs. 32.5%

To add a little insult to the injury already inflicted, Reagan Consulting did a study of how producers are produced.

From that they designed an infographic from which these stats were pulled. (You can find that infographic at www.thewedge.net/RCinfo)

Here's the bottom line… according to the research:

- The overall success rate is 56%, but the bottom 25% of agencies only had a new producer success rate of 22%.

That means they have to hire 5 new producers to have 1 success.

- This stat will blow your mind: 55% of hires were experienced producers, 'free agents moving from one firm to another', robbing Peter to grow Paul. Careful, you might be rearranging the chairs on the Titanic if you are hiring experienced producers (maybe someone else's rejects).

- This stat drives the charts you see above: 55-60% of firms are 'under-hiring'. They are not hiring enough to support their desired growth rates. What does that mean? It means you are planning your agency's death by not hiring producers. You might as well call your M&A consultant, get a sell date on the calendar; it's inevitable.

Here's a new term you'll want to learn: The Average Weighted Age of Shareholders. By the way, that number is 53.3 years old. The Average Weighted Age of Producers is 48.7. The bad news is this; both weighted average numbers have gone up 2 years in the last 5. That's a very bad trend and it's validated in the charts.

What's the solution? Hire New Producers...

What IS your New Producer Hiring Process?

Have you seen this happen recently?

You decide you want to hire a new producer and get on the growth bandwagon at your agency. Good decision.

To find new candidates, you either contract with a recruiter (about $10,000 a pop) or someone on your team tells you about a client that has a sharp son; he just graduated college a few years ago and he's out looking.

Regardless of how you sourced, them… there he is. He's a fairly good-looking young guy, friendly, nice and has a warm personality.

You interview the guy and like him well enough, so you introduce him to your other partners; everybody gets the chance to meet him.

A couple of weeks later, you're having a board meeting and you ask: *"What did you think of him?"* Almost everyone agrees that he seems like a nice young guy, everyone except Tom. And Tom got his name honestly because he's a doubting Thomas… always skeptical. You ask your partners, *"Do you think we should give him a shot?"* Everyone except Tom answers, *"Why not?"*

So there you go: *"Let's hire the guy."*

Before you hire him, you decide to do a personality profile. You've never been a big fan of those personality profiles. You took one at an early part of your career - it wasn't too complimentary - but, look how successful you are now.

Oh well, it seems like a formality you should consider, even though it does cost $175. So you set him up to get tested.

Once it's done, they forward you a copy of the results. And, as you review all of the psychological mumbo jumbo, it says in small print: '*Hire, with reservations.*'

What does that mean, hire with reservations? It means he might be good and he might not. Caveat Emptor - buyer beware.

Since everyone at the board meeting, except Tom, has agreed to hire him and the profile didn't exactly say you should take a pass -- you hire him, with fingers crossed, thinking: *"I hope this kid can make it."*

He's Hired - First Things First

Now that he's hired, you get him over to the HR department, and they do their job. There's an agency orientation, they have him sign some documents, give him an agency handbook and set him up with a nice cubical and a computer.

Someone else steps in to help him get licensed. Then he takes a nice little trip to Connecticut, where some of the world's largest insurance carriers provide low-cost, new producer training. Having completed all of that in a whirlwind tour, he is now ready to produce.

Three Months In

It's been about three months, so you peek in to check on him. Not a lot is going on. He's not burning up the phone setting appointments. You're able to rationalize it by saying; "*He's new, give him a chance.*"

Six Months In

Six months in he's got a little activity going on, he's written some really small accounts, but he's not on his validation track, nowhere near it in fact. You're wondering, was this a good decision?

58

Nine Months In

Nine months into his employment, you're still forking out his salary every month. And because you feel sorry for the kid, you make sure he is getting all of the call-in leads, hoping he'll book enough revenue to make it. You hope it will all add up to building some confidence.

Not Sleeping Well

One morning you wake up from a non-restful sleep and it is only 4:00 am. You ask yourself: *"What am I doing? Why am I thinking about this?"* After a huge sigh, you decide to get up. *"Holy crap, what is going on with this kid?"*

You stumble out of bed and into the kitchen. You put on a pot of coffee and then head to your study. There you get out your yellow pad and a calculator and start thinking through: *"What am I spending on this guy?"*

Coffee pot beeps, you're back in the kitchen, grabbing a cup, then back to the study as you settle in and start calculating: *"What's his salary?"* You're probably paying him $50,000. *"What are benefits costing us?"* That could be another $5,000 right there.

And then, *"How much have we paid for his training?"* You add that all up, maybe that's $10,000 with travel and expenses.

How do you put a number on all of the time invested in this kid by the staff? You wing it.

As you reflect over the past 9 months, you recall that every time you ask him how many calls he's made, he just tells you: *"I'm making a lot."*

But you know you're not getting real answers. You don't even know if he's really making calls. And you're not sure how many appointments he's been on. What if he's not really working that hard?

When you've asked: *"Do you have any opportunities to quote coming up?"* Of course, he always says he's working on a few deals, but you're sure it's not enough. And so far, he hasn't sold anything except some really small accounts.

As you reflect you wonder: *"What's the potential of this kid?"* If you are honest with yourself, you know there's no way he's going to make it. This was a mistake. He doesn't have the activity. He's not driven to make it happen.

So you conclude that you'll bring him into your office today, have a big boy talk and probably let him know that you don't think this is the right fit for him.

He's A Happy Camper... But, Are You?

You show up at the office about 8:30 am. About 9:00, you pick up your phone, you ask the young guy to come in and have a seat, and you say, *"How's it going?"*

And much to your surprise, he goes, *"Oh, it's great."*

You respond, *"Really, what's going on?"*

"Well, I met with a guy yesterday afternoon. You wouldn't believe it – great prospect, about $12,000 in revenue. He's not happy with his current guy. I think we've got a great chance of getting this deal."

Now, you're sitting there thinking to yourself, *"Man, I need to put a bullet in this dude, but he just showed a little bit of life, a little bit of hope. I guess I'll give him a chance."*

So you say, *"Okay. Well, good luck. Please keep me in the loop and let me know how it's going. If you need some help, let me know."*

Chapter 3 – How to Hire Great Producers
(Challenge #2)

What happens then? Well, you get really busy and two months fly by and you never hear from him. Now, you're 11 months into the gig and you're thinking, "Holy crap, what's going on?"

He didn't say anything about it, so you call him back in. *"Remember a couple of months ago, you told me about that $12,000 deal?"*

"Well yeah, I remember. Too bad that it didn't happen, but I've got another one. I met with a guy last week; it's almost $30,000 in revenue." And then here comes the same story, just different characters.

If you're not careful, instead of firing him, you continue to take money out of your pocket and put money into his pocket; unfortunately, he can't sell or won't sell.

It's a tough situation; it happens to almost everybody. If you don't change your hiring process, you'll keep this cycle going. Not only does it break your heart and empty your bank account, it can have a nasty impact on your confidence.

If you don't fix this problem, growing your agency organically is almost a pipedream.

Pipedream: An unattainable or fanciful hope or scheme.

6 Critical Success Factors for Finding, Recruiting, Hiring, Training and Developing New Producers

You agree that hiring new producers should not be a crapshoot any more than writing a new account. There are specific things you need to do to qualify an account. And, there are specific things you need to do to qualify a new producer.

Here are 6 MUST-HAVE characteristics EVERY new producer should bring to the table and, if not... **Do. Not. Hire. Them.**

1. The Ability to deal with Rejection

The biggest problem, not the only problem, but the **biggest** problem that causes producers to fail, is a lack of prospecting activity. You saw it in the real example above.

And, the #1 cause is <u>fear of rejection</u>. As a result, they won't pick up the phone, they won't network with the right people and they won't knock on doors.

When they have this problem, they have NO ONE to sell to, except for call-ins, friends and family.

So, get out your check-list and put that as #1.

2. They Have To Be Street Smart

What is street smart? It's more than a good GPA. It's the ability to figure things out and to field the curve balls.

If not, they'll never break down a policy. They won't learn your services. They won't get what they need from an underwriter. They won't get beyond the receptionist. They won't be able to deal with tough prospects, and there are a lot of tough, manipulative prospects, aren't there?

Another way to say this is Emotional Quotient (EQ); it's the ability to be a chameleon, to dance when your prospects dance, to be gruff when needed, to be bold or soft. It's the ability to adapt to your surroundings… that is street smart; that is EQ.

3. Driven- Something to Prove

The word 'Drive' encompasses so many things. But you'll know if someone has DRIVE, because they will find a way to get things done, even if that means they have to run over you, around you or through you. Hopefully they will run with you, but they will find a way to get it done.

There is also an economic 'DRIVE' that is extraordinarily important. The insurance industry is full of producers making $125,000 a year. When producers hit that number, the majority of them go on auto-pilot, instead of putting the pedal to the metal. Since they aren't economically driven, they will quit when they make enough money to survive.

4. Great At Relationships

If they have all of those characteristics, but they are not likable… they will fail.

A successful producer must be able to cause others to feel important, to be a great listener and speaker, and to be able to engage a prospect effectively.

5. Resilient- They Bounce Off of Walls

This might sound like I am describing Spiderman, but I'm not. Here's the problem -- the insurance business is tough, particularly for the first 2-4 years. There are bad days, bad weeks, bad months and sometimes even bad years.

One day an underwriter pulls back their quote. The next day a prospect backs out of their commitment, because the incumbent begged and pleaded for them to stay. The day after that, a confirmed appointment calls to cancel. Next you find out your support person is pregnant and you feel helpless. And it can get much worse.

So resilience is key… the ability to get up and charge the wall again and again. If they are not resilient, they will quit. They will quit working. They'll quit prospecting. They will just quit trying hard.

There are a lot of good people, who are smart. They're good at relationships and appear to deal well with rejection, but in the long run, they just can't handle the stress and they quit.

You must determine if they are resilient BEFORE you hire them.

6. Coachable

Have you ever worked with someone, who wasn't coachable? They were resistant, hard-headed, stubborn, headstrong, uncooperative, immovable… need I go on?

It's good to have a strong-minded producer, but when you get someone who isn't coachable, they won't learn from their mistakes. It makes life miserable for you and them.

Hire These 6 Characteristics and Your Life Will Get Easier

The biggest problem with hiring new producers is that you never know what you got until after you hire them. Clearly, no one would get hired, if you didn't believe they would make it. But the stats speak to a different outcome. 50% of new hires are failures, even when hiring someone with experience.

When YOU get this figured out, your life will get easier and here is why: Talent makes heroes of us all.

For a resource on how to determine if your new producer candidate has what it takes to be successful, before you hire them - not after - go here for a free ebook on Hiring New Producers: www.thewedge.net/newproducerguide

Chapter 4

No Time to Lead Sales (Challenge #3)

What happens when you put a self-directed team in the game against a well-coached team? 8 times out of 10, if the talent is similar, the well-coached team will win. Why is that?

If the coach is doing his job, he'll manage the resources better. He'll motivate his players. He'll match up his strengths to gain the advantage. He'll pull players out when they get tired and give them a rest. He'll change the defense to stop a dominant player on their team, while setting up offensive plays to gain a scoring advantage.

In most cases, a self-directed team will not do that.

If there is no coach, two-thirds of the players will be screwing around, while a couple of guys are busting their butts.

When there is no coach, there is probably no playbook for offense or defense. When that's the case, a few dominant players will hog the ball on offense, doing their shake and bake, 1 on 5 drill-darting to the basket... and throwing up low-percentage shots. And on defense, no one gets back on a fast-break to prevent easy scores.

This kind of team, although talented, would probably get beat 8 out of 10 times by a well-coached team.

Sports Teams need leadership and so do Sales Teams -- IF they are to ever reach their full potential.

Leading a sales team in an agency is a problem for the agency owner and here are three reasons why:

The First Problem: You have an Agency to Run

As Agency Owner, you have an agency to run. If you're fortunate, you've got a great support staff to handle all the day-to-day activities of running a company. If you're not so fortunate, you'll soon feel like you've been drawn and quartered.

You have a lot of responsibilities:
- Personnel decisions
- Underwriter & carrier meetings
- Shareholder meetings

- Strategic planning sessions

The bottom line is that a substantial part of your day is roped, harnessed and ridden into the sunset -- a huge chunk that you will never get back.

The Second Problem: You Have a Personal Book to Grow

It's common knowledge, that a lot of your personal income is derived from your own personal production, unless you are running a major league agency and are the majority stockholder.

That clearly means one thing: Your book is your lifeline, and as such, you must make it TOP priority. You have to handle renewals, get involved in nasty claim messes, engage with underwriters, fight off competitors, write new business and grow your book. It is the easiest and fastest route to greater personal income.

Agency Owners generally fall into one of these buckets:

Either you're a born salesman and love meeting with clients, building your book -- sell, sell, sell. It's just fun.

Or, you love the mechanics of the business; the operations. Getting your fingers in the overall planning and execution is the place where you derive a lot of work satisfaction.

Either way, you make a lot of your money from managing your book of business and that leaves a big gap on the sales frontier as very few Agency Owners love rolling up their sleeves and leading sales.

The Third Problem: Not Enough Time or Resources to Develop Your Sales Team

You run sales meetings and wish they were better, but you don't have a lot of time to plan for them. You're always willing to help a producer strategize on difficult accounts if asked. You conduct an annual goal setting and planning session with your producers.

You are involved with your sales team, but it's like being a player coach much more than a head coach.

You don't feel you have enough time to devote to it. And you don't have systems in place to support it where you can train others to help you. So the biggest part of the burden is on your shoulders.

Ultimately the problem is you don't have time, or you don't make it a priority, and you have a self-directed sales team. That's not a problem if they are all studs… but if they aren't, that's the recipe for mediocrity.

Consider this truth:

The difference between where your firm is today and where it will be 5 years from now -- is in direct proportion to YOUR ABILITY to develop your sales team.

What does that mean?

It means, if your firm isn't growing at the pace you want, you don't have a producer problem, YOU HAVE A LEADERSHIP PROBLEM.

When you invest a little time and money in developing YOUR ABILITY to grow and develop your producers, they will grow and develop. If you leave it up to them and their own devices, the majority of them will do what people naturally do; take the easy road.

If you want to get excited about the potential of growth, play three 'what-if' games. Get your partners in the boardroom and using the whiteboard, map out these scenarios:

Chapter 4 – No Time to Lead Sales
(Challenge #3)

The first game is pretty simple; assume nothing really changes, project how big each producer's book will be in 5 years based upon their current and past performance. Will you be happy with that?

The second game is to assume YOU can step-up and get your Middle 60% of producers on a steeper growth path by training, developing and coaching them to prospect more and write bigger accounts; where does that put you?

The third game; do what you did in the second game, while adding new producers SUCCESSFULLY each year for the next 5 years and determine where that would put you.

The big difference between where your agency is now and where it will be five years from now is in YOUR ABILITY to develop your sales team, to get more out of the existing players (which is in their best interest) and add new producers successfully.

When you look at it objectively, you have four types of producers.

1. **High Performers:** They meet or exceed their new business goals every year.

2. **High Potentials:** They have talent, but it hasn't been developed to benefit you or them. As a result, they are keepers, but not performing anywhere near their full potential.

3. **Legacy:** These producers have been in the business a long time. They came up under the belief that the book of business they manage is theirs, not the agency's, that they can do what they want, when they want. They are like independent contractors… not a real part of a growing team. They are sometimes referred to as the 'walking dead'. Is there any growth potential here? Yes, but you need a strategy if you really want to harvest it.

4. **Newbies:** These producers are new, unvalidated producers. They are a big drain on cash-flow, but an important investment in the future of the agency. They are the source of your BIG growth, but to get that, they must be trained, coached and developed. That takes a lot of time and resources.

You want to help them, and you know that by doing so it helps you and your partners.

Your desire is there, but TIME is short. And if you are like 7 out of 10 Agency Owners, you begin, right at this point, talking yourself out of it: You are too busy, there is too much to learn, your producers won't respond, your partners will run and hide… and you feel you are left on an island to fend for yourself.

To accomplish your financial and growth goals, you must help your producers accomplish their financial and growth goals. But, you don't have a goal setting system, you have basic spreadsheets. You don't have a prospecting and sales training system; you just tell them to try harder. You don't have a central prospect management system; everyone manages their prospects their own way. You don't have a quality sales meeting format; it's the "liars' club". You don't have a process for differentiation; you tell them to sell themselves. You have no repository of your competitors or copies of their proposals; it's just in everyone's head. You've hired new producers, but you don't have a process that enables you to separate the pretenders from real producers. And when they do get hired, you don't have a way to onboard and train them to win; they for the most part fend for themselves.

It's a mess and the thought of starting from scratch is enough to make you want to turn the other way and keep doing what you've been doing. It's an easy justification: *"We're making money, we're not that bad."*

Please don't justify mediocrity, if that's what is happening. And don't lose hope.

I'll show you a system in the next few chapters that, when you implement it, takes the pressure off of your shoulders and helps to transfer it to a bigger team with assistant coaches.

And, when you adopt this step-by-step process, you'll conquer your 3 biggest growth challenges.

3 Biggest Challenges to Growth:

1. How to Motivate the Bottom 80% of Your Producers to Produce.
2. How to Find, Hire and Develop New Producers into Million Dollar Producers.
3. How to Get it DONE, very efficiently with only a Minimal Amount of Time.

Chapter 5

The 5-Step Process to Extraordinary Growth

It took 22 years of thinking about it, experimenting with it, training it, changing it, tweaking it, teaching it, training it some more and getting lots of feedback to develop this organic growth system.

Frankly, it's been anything but easy... but, if you've been struggling with how YOU can create an Organic Growth Machine, with how to Drive Your Sales Culture forward... then you're not alone.

There are a lot of agencies struggling to figure it out.

So, let's dive in.

Step #1: Commit to Growth

Is there anything you have in your life that is really good, that didn't take a genuine commitment? Probably not.

Why aren't more agencies growing at a faster pace?

The only plausible answer is relatively simple. They just never committed.

Maybe they started, gave it some effort, and then quit. It just got too hard. It's like a diet. You don't quit eating; you just stop eating healthy. Maybe it's their golf game? They didn't quit playing golf; they just dropped the lessons and never got any better?

No one is saying Agency Owners quit talking about sales; but they quit DRIVING sales. BIG difference!

There is no Magic Pill or a Secret Formula. And there will always be a problem producer or two. But the real reason 7 out of 10 Agency Owners quit is... They never really committed.

COWARDS never start.
THE WEAK never finish.
WINNERS never quit!

If you really want to grow your agency and solve the 3 BIG challenges we discussed, it takes a 'Winners Never Quit' commitment.

To make this fun, exciting, and to gain buy-in from your producers, there are a couple of really important things you will want to commit to.

Here they are:

Part 1: Commit To Being a Proactive Services Firm - Providing A Unique and Differentiated Client Experience.

Your firm is in business to serve clients. When you do that extraordinarily well, they reward you with long-term loyalty. And you know having a loyal client base opens the door for big time organic growth.

How do you differentiate your service from that of your competitors? Most agencies have mastered their reactive services capability, which means they are good at things like getting out certificates, returning phones calls and emails, and checking policies for accuracy.

Why is having a Proactive Services Platform important to agency growth? Here is the primary reason. Your best producers can sell in any environment; they just have the DNA to figure it out. They will make money working at your firm, but they will probably do just as well regardless of where they go. You just have to admit, they have something special.

But for the average producer, who frankly doesn't have that 'something special', they need an edge. Where will they get that edge?

Is it better reactive service? Probably not; your competitors do a pretty good job at that.

Is it better pricing? Probably not; most of your competitors have access to the same or similar markets and they can match or get close to the pricing.

Is it better coverage? Doubt it.

The average producer has lower close rates, writes smaller accounts and produces less new business. And it's not that having Proactive Services will solve all of their problems by any means, But, it IS the foundational 'differentiating' factor that allows them to beat the incumbent. Unless your producers DO something, that clients don't even know to ask for – but after seeing it, can't live without – then your guys are just like the other guys. And, there is a good chance they will get rolled.

When you can help them build confidence around this concept, you can develop Ninja-like sales people.

If you don't, they'll have to rely on traditional selling techniques, which are based upon relationship, finding a coverage gap, getting a cheaper price and hoping to win the business.

To differentiate yourself from the agency that does a good job with reactive service and has similar markets to you, you need to provide Proactive Services that are clearly defined, easy to explain and can help control the cost of insurance for your clients.

Confidence Breeds Success

When you train your producers to sell using Proactive Service, their confidence goes up, their energy peaks, their desire to engage in the hand to hand combat of winning an account increases, their ability to get a BOR soars and it has the impact you really want; an inspired sales team that is growing.

If Not, Meet the **Elephant**

Imagine you are the incumbent agent and some agent is coming after your account, what are you going to do?

When an agent is coming after your account using traditional sales techniques (price/coverage/relationship), you will leverage your relationship with your client to get the last look.

And with that, you match the coverage and price and keep the business. The guy, using traditional selling techniques, JUST GOT ROLLED. And that is why the average producer, using traditional selling techniques, working at a reactive services firm, has such low closing rates.

You have to change the game, if you want to dominate.

How do you do that?

You need to put your average producers in a Proactive Sales Culture.

Then, you need to teach them how to use Ninja tactics and Proactive Services to get the prospect to discover the incumbent isn't doing their job.

That's when the whole game changes.

The Average producer is then able to WIN more accounts and bigger accounts. And do so, often, by AOR/BOR.

Now isn't that a shift worth considering? It all starts with your commitment to be a Proactive Services Firm.

A Quick Test

Do you want to know if your agency is a Proactive Services Firm?

It's easy to find out.

Simply ask your producers or one of your support staff to pull up the Written Service Plan for each of your agency's Top Clients.

As you analyze that Written Service Plan that your client has initialed as something important to them, you'll want to look for concrete, specific deliverables... such as Claims Reviews, Mod-Projections, Payroll Analysis, Business Interruption Limits Review, etc. There could be more or less items depending on the size and complexity of the account.

But the point is, that if a Written Service Plan does NOT exist, and yet your producers 'feel' like they are being Proactive, then their feelings are misleading them, aren't they?

If you feel like an NBA basketball player, but your history doesn't bear that out; if you can't dunk on an NBA big man, if you can't dribble into the paint and get off a shot, if you can't defend an NBA guard, then you're probably not NBA material, regardless of your feelings.

The same is true with your producers; they might feel they are being proactive, but if they don't have documentation and a system to back it up, it's only a feeling.

It's simple; with a Proactive Services Platform, you not only deliver a Unique and Differentiated Client Experience, you give your producers concrete tools to win new business.

Part 2: Commit to Your Producers - Help Your Producers Double their Personal Income

After you commit to being a Proactive Services Firm and setting the foundation for a differentiated client experience, if you want serious organic growth, you need to think about your producers.

What do your producers need?

Think about this, how many of your producers legitimately NEED to double their personal income?

How many of them need to make twice as much money as they make now, to not only pay their living expenses, but to save a tremendous amount so they can fund cars, university tuitions and weddings for their kids.

They also NEED to make a lot more money to be able to save a lot for their own retirement, so they can live without worry when they hang up their producer hat.

Do they want to Double Their Personal Income?

I'm sure they do if you ask, but are they DRIVEN to Double Their Personal Income? Probably not.

Why not?

Producers are simply ignorant about how much money it will take to fund their future financial obligations. They do NOT understand how much money it's going to take.

Most people, insurance producers included, are woefully unprepared for their future. Everything revolves around money, but they are not taught that in our education system.

So, even those who've earned a degree most likely don't know how much they need to save annually and for how many years to accomplish their life goals. As a result, they are just doing what they feel is the best they can. But, they can do better than that and here is why.

I Was One of Those Ignorant Guys

Today I have 4 daughters, who are 23, 21, 19 and 16.

It was literally 17 years ago that my kids were 6, 4, 2 and soon to be born.

I was running a sales meeting in Houston, Texas at an agency client of mine. We started at 8:00 a.m. and were 30 minutes into our meeting when Paul arrived. Paul was always on time; being late was very unusual for him.

As he slipped into the room, he apologized for being late and interrupting what was going on.

I acknowledged him and politely asked: *"Everything ok?"*

He replied: *"Yes, sorry, I got in really late last night and slept in an extra hour."*

"What time did you get in?" I asked.

He said it was about 4:30 a.m.

That's pretty late, so I asked, *"What was going on that you were out until 4:30 in the morning?"*

And that is when the story began.

Basically, he did what all college parents do. He rented a U-Haul trailer, packed his daughter's furniture and clothes inside and headed off for college. That college happened to be Texas Tech in Lubbock, Texas, about an 11-hour drive from Houston.

After getting her all set up, he made a beeline back to Houston. The unfortunate part is that it took considerably longer than he expected and he got in really late.

After he told me that part of the story, I asked: *"Any other kids in school?"*

"Yes', he said, and then told me about a second daughter, who was a couple of years ahead of this one.

It was at that point, I looked him right in the eye and said: *"The good news is that it's all paid for, isn't it?"*

He lowered his head and shook it side to side, indicating his daughters' education was not already paid for; in fact he was funding it month to month out of his income.

My Holy Crap Moment

You talk about financially ignorant! I'm sitting there in a bit of a daze, as I started to think about the FACT that I have 4 daughters. And it became crystal clear to me that I didn't have a clue how much money I would need to save to pay for cars, college and weddings – not to mention my own retirement.

Most of the people I grew up around never thought about this either. And the biggest reason was, that there wasn't much they could do about it. They were all blue-collar workers or farmers. Everyone was doing the best they could to get by; no one had any extra money lying around, nor did they have the ability to make more money. In fact, we all felt lucky if we could take a vacation about every 4-5 years.

Talking Money… Taboo

And of course it's taboo - even to this day - to talk about money. If you make a lot a lot of money, most people feel you shouldn't talk about it; you'll be seen as bragging. You can hear it now from your mother and father: "No one needs to know how much money we make; it's our business - not theirs."

All of that leads to a lot of financial ignorance for most people.

Do YOUR producers need to make TWICE as much money than they're currently making?

You know the Middle 60 percenters definitely do. **DO THEY KNOW IT?** They know in general. Do they have a plan? No, they don't.

And, that is what's driving their new production goal setting; a big ol' general 'Don't Know'.

This Is Your Opportunity to Make a Difference for You and Them

Let's start with one basic assumption… your producers are not dummies. They have way more capability than they're tapping into, I'm sure of it. For the most part, they (like most people) are letting fear, apprehension and apathy control their lives… instead of courage, desire and ambition.

Can you make their fear and apprehension go away? No, you can't.

Can you make them brave, courageous and ambitious? No, you can't.

Can you influence it in a powerful way? Yes, you can.

It starts with giving them a Financial Education. And how long should your financial education strategy last? Forever is the only plausible answer.

Let's do this really fast.

Invite one of your middle 60 percenters, just an average producer, into your office. Below are the questions you want to ask him. Write down his/her answer or ask them to write it down.

1. *"I suppose that someday you want to retire. Do you know how much money you need to have saved at that point to last until the day you die, so you don't have to worry or stress about money?"*

There is a high probability they will have a very general number because they don't know. The number should be 22 times their annual spend at retirement age. So, if they want to retire on $100,000 a year, they need to have $2,200,000 in their retirement account.

If they can't answer that question, they are doomed on all the rest, but keep going anyway.

2. *"In order to have that much money saved at retirement age, how much do you have to save every year until then?"*

They won't know. They will give one of those fuzzy answers like *"We're just going to do the best we can."*

3. *"How big does your book of business have to get, so it will throw off enough money for you to pay all your bills and be able to save that much money every year?"*

They won't know. And about now, they are feeling really uncomfortable and embarrassed. But, don't let their discomfort cause you to stop. **This is SO fundamentally important to their success and the growth of your agency. Please do not stop.**

4. *"In order to grow a book of business that big in the next 3-5 years, how much new business do you have to write every year to get yourself there?"*

They won't know. If they don't know, you have to ask yourself, what is driving them to write new business? And what should scare the crap out of you is this; they are writing enough new business to NOT GO BACKWARDS, or maybe advance just a little bit.

Is that the basis for a robust Sales Culture? Will that get this agency on the path of double-digit or at least high single digit growth? No, it will not.

Is that a producer problem or a LEADERSHIP problem? You can blame your producers all you want, but they are a product of the culture YOU BUILT.

Here is what this means to your agency. Your #1 resource for growth, for writing new business for slaying the incumbent, for selling your agency proposition… they don't have clear, concise, personal goals that drive them. What would happen if you made an adjustment in your process to fix this? What would be the financial impact for you and for them over the next five years? Can you say HUGE?

Sincerely Speaking

This is not a farce, a setup, a con or manipulation of any sort.

If you genuinely care about your producers and their families, you could really help them with this. Imagine the pride you would have, saying to your friends, peers, clients or spouse: "We intentionally plan to help every one of our producers become financially independent."

Think about that from a branding perspective. If your firm was committed to helping **ALL** your producers double their personal incomes, save a tremendous amount of money and become financially independent… what do you think would happen to the reputation of your firm?

Can you say, 'Pick of the litter'?

Can you envision how star quality recruits would be banging down your door to have a chance to join your firm?

Do you think that might make your recruiting easier? Do you think you'd attract the best of the best? Would there be a spike in energy level at your agency?

Is there anything negative about creating an environment that inspires, encourages, educates and motivates producers to gain real clarity about their financial future - then provide them a proven path to go get it?

And when you do this... what's in it for you? Simply put, when a producer doubles his/her personal income, they just doubled their book. When they double their book, the value of your agency goes up too.

There is nothing but WIN/WIN in this concept.

So the second part of the Commitment is simply this: Commit to Helping Every Producer You Have Double Their Personal Income in 3-5 years.

Summary: COMMITMENT TO GROWTH

Extraordinary Growth requires two very important things:

1. A sincere commitment to being a Proactive Services Firm that Creates a Unique and Differentiated Customer Experience. This gives your producers something quantitative to sell; not just fluff.

2. A commitment to drive and support producers in your agency to Double their Personal Income in 3-5 years with only half the accounts. **This helps all your producers accomplish their personal goals, making this a producer centric culture, a WIN/WIN.**

Now, let's deal with the second part of that statement: Double their personal income in 3-5 years with:

HALF THE ACCOUNTS.

With HALF THE ACCOUNTS is foundational to building the rest of your Agency's Organic Growth Culture.

And, like any good foundation, it MUST be done. Here is why it is not optional, if you want to experience exponential growth and be in the position to dominate your market.

Time is the one commodity that we all have in common. You and everyone you know we're all blessed with 24 hours a day. It is the great equalizer. How you and your producers use that time has everything to do with how fast their personal income will grow and how fast your agency will grow.

When your producers and their support staff use their time to service, manage and renew SMALL accounts, they aren't using it to write, service and manage LARGER accounts. It becomes painfully obvious if you are willing to consider the facts.

Look at this research one more time: It's not rocket science.

There were 168 producers with just under $92 million in revenue and that represented 17,808 commercial accounts.

The analysis broke their books of business into three sections; the Top 20%, the Middle 40% and the Bottom 40%.

Here is the summary:

The average book had 106 accounts, averaging $5,159 in revenue for a total of $546,857

73% of their revenue, or $399,702, came from 21 accounts - the Top 20% and averaged $17,773 per account.

4% of their revenue, $22,303, came from 43 accounts - the Bottom 40% and averaged $518 per account.

Being very analytical and critical at the same time, if you were the consultant, what would you see in these numbers?

First off, you'd ask how much time is involved for the support staff to service the $22,303 of revenue that comes from the bottom 43 accounts that produce an average of $518 of agency revenue. How many hours are involved in renewing these accounts? Is paying a producer to retain this business profitable for the agency and good for the producer?

If you look at it from a producer's perspective you'd ask the question this way. Let's use 30% as the renewal commission.

On just one of the larger accounts valued at an average of $17,703, a producer makes $5,310. On just one of the bottom accounts, $518, a producer makes $155.

A producer makes 34 times more money from one large account than they do from one of their small accounts. Said another way, a producer would have to write 34 small accounts to equate what just one of the larger accounts would provide in personal income. Then they have to renew 34 small accounts to retain that revenue. It's a lot of work and very little money.

What's worse is, that the support staff is so overwhelmed with dealing with all the small accounts, that they can't focus on the larger accounts the way they should. Then what happens? The producer is no longer a producer; they become an executive level CSR or member of the support staff, because their team can't keep up with all the minutiae. When that happens, the producer no longer produces, which means their personal income is capped. And it means that your #1 asset to grow your agency, your producer force, is out of business… no longer a producer, but an account manager.

There's nothing earth shattering about these observations - just a very pragmatic way of looking at the problem of sustainable growth in an agency environment.

Step #1 has outlined what you have to commit to, if you want to grow your agency. You have to commit to growth, because there will be obstacles and you will want to quit. If you are committed, you won't quit. Then you have to commit to being a Proactive Services firm, because it turns your value proposition into something tangible, something real. It gives your producers something concrete to sell, instead of fluff. That builds their confidence to be in the market prospecting and selling. Next you have to get all of the small accounts out of your producers' books of business. They will argue that it doesn't take any of their time, but for the most part they are delusional; it does take time. And since we only have 24 hours, the person that learns how to get the most from their time wins the game.

What would cause a producer to want to do this? You have to get them clear on what their financial future will look like if they do and if they don't. Remove the ambiguity, get to the facts. College tuition will cost $100,000 to $200,000. Weddings cost from $15,000 to $75,000. The retirement fund needs 22x whatever they plan to live on until they die. It could range from $1,000,000 all the way up to $3,500,000 and maybe more.

If they aren't saving $50,000 to $100,000 a year, for approximately 20 years, they are way underfunded.

It is the producer's intrinsic motivation -- the desire to do what's best for him and his family -- combined with a very specific plan for how to make it happen that will help change your agency into a Growth Machine. When you can find a way to perpetually tap into that, and you can do it through Financial Education, you've taken a very big step toward creating an Agency Growth Machine.

Step #2: You Can't Drive an Idea - You Must Have a Process

Now you've committed to developing an Agency Growth Machine. You want it, your partners want it, and your producers want it. Everyone sees and feels how this is in their best interest.

What now?

If you were a college coach, you'd need a playbook for your players to learn and implement. As a Sales Coach, you need the same.

Why is that important?

If you don't have a playbook - something that details what you want your producers to do - how are you going to drive it? Without a playbook all that is left are good ideas. How are you going to communicate and drive that? You can't.

It's like standing on the corner of a street and saying: *"You can all be wealthy"*. Then someone says to you, *"How do we do it?"* If you answer with, *"Just work smart, do the best you can,"* then they have every right to look at you like you're nuts.

But if you said: *"I have a plan, a process... it's proven. Let me show it to you.'* How different would that be?

The same is true with your producers. You can't just say, *"Let's go double your personal incomes,"* without a plan, a playbook or a business process.

That makes this step huge for you and them. Without a plan you can't drive it. Without a plan, they have nothing to believe in.

Let me show you a playbook. It's a plan that is proven daily, by over 1,000 active producers our firm is coaching now.

The Flight Plan

I started using the Flight Plan analogy for two reasons. It has a visual component that everyone can easily understand. And it demonstrates the point, precisely.

Selling is Like Flying. If you don't land safely, nothing else really matters. So, with selling… the successful outcome is making the sale.

But what can prevent your safe landing/sale? Well, there can be a lot of things, but very often the culprit is… the incumbent.

Imagine this… you're coming in for a landing and are about to put your wheels on the runway (get the sale). But just before you land, the incumbent is watching you through her binoculars and just moments before your wheels touch the runway, she pulls up the bazooka and blows you out of the sky.

It's called getting rolled. And you know it happens all the time. In fact, every time someone comes after your accounts, you don't just play dead and let them have it, do you? No, you use whatever ammo you have in your arsenal to prevent them from landing safely and taking your account away from you.

You probably use all sorts of tactics, including playing the guilt card, the loyalty card, the "Look at all the things we've done for you over the past couple of years" card. And no one can blame you -- it's just part of the game. Always has been and always will be as long as insurance is sold by people and not machines.

So a safe landing is analogous to making the sale – to getting the new account and ultimately, growing a huge book of business.

Let's take a look at every step of the Flight Plan.

In the office (hangar) – you're performing Proactive Service Maintenance. This prevents accidents, mishaps or an all-out CRASH… where you lose the account to another agent. You prevent that, with a Written Service Timeline, co-created with your client.

1. Red Hot Introductions -- when you've done a good job of Proactively Servicing your accounts, you've earned the right to ask for and receive an introduction to someone they know. That is the source of your very best prospects. Having the Written Service Timeline in place takes away the fear and angst associated with asking for that introduction. This step leads to a quality appointment with a new prospect.

2. Precall strategy – the equivalent to a Pre-Flight prep for a pilot. You have to figure out where you want to go, check the weather, check your fuel, project flight time and submit a flight plan. Same is true with Pre-call Strategy. You have a

destination in mind, but for you to land safely, you have to deal with the incumbent.

The incumbent must get fired for you to get hired. In the pre-call strategy, you research your prospect and their potential needs, by understanding who is serving them now. Who is the incumbent and what is s/he doing and not doing? Lastly, you must build a strategy to bust the incumbent relationship.

3. The Wedge -- a selling model to bust the incumbent relationship and get your competition fired. Using information gained in the pre-call strategy, you now go on the sales call and leverage your differentiation in a powerful way to cause your prospect to discover they have needs that are not being met by the incumbent.

You co-create a solution and get that confirmed. Then you rehearse the prospect through the process of firing the incumbent. Having completed those steps, you now move on to either getting a BOR/AOR or marketing the account to the insurance companies.

4. Pre-close; then present your proposal. This step is called Keystone, because it's analogous to the Keystone put in all the ancient arches to lock all the other pieces in place.

The biggest risk at this point of the sales process is the relationship that the incumbent has with their client/your prospect. If you're not careful, the ambitious and clever incumbent will find a way to match your price, match your coverage and match the services you say you can provide. The purpose of this step is to preempt that and win the business.

5. Wedge-proof the account -- by installing a Co-Created Written Service Plan, the client is assured he's getting exactly what he said he wants, but isn't getting from his current agent.

6. Cross-sell the account by getting your associate into the account to write other lines of business.

These steps represent your Flight Plan. It is NOT nebulous. Nor is it left to chance or whims. It's a process to be followed to WIN business and grow a book. And the whole point of laying that out for you is this: If you don't have a well-defined process -- a playbook – it will be next to impossible to take your agency to another level of growth.

Without a standard guidebook, everyone is doing their own thing. Some will be efficient and effective, but many won't. It's hit or miss. And that, like hope, is NOT a strategy, is it?

Let me ask you, have you ever built a new home? If so, did you have a blueprint for the new home you wanted to build? I bet you said yes. There is a simple reason for that: If you don't have a blueprint, the builder would have to guess what you want. The chance they could 'guess' accurately is pretty low, isn't it? Knowing that a new home is going to cost anywhere from $250,000 up to over a Million, that's a pretty big risk to take.

The same is true when making a decision to drive your sales culture. The value of a well-run sales team versus a group of producers doing their own thing could easily be worth millions, depending on the size of the team.

Without a blueprint or a playbook, how are you going to drive your team to double their personal incomes and double your agency?

You might be thinking that it wouldn't matter how good the blueprint is, how much training you do, how great a leader you are; there is no way your producers will respond. And you might be right. If you are right, you just locked yourself into a prison of hopelessness.

However, you might be one of the 3 out of 10 that gets it. Changing your agency is a process. It takes a well-defined strategy that can be implemented and improved over time.

Some producers will get it quickly; some will take time. And along the way, you'll add more new producers to the mix. One year from now you'll be better off than you are today and 5 years from now it'll be a different shop.

As you go through this process, you will continue to shift your attitude about your producers being too old to change, too professional to get better or too hopeless for you to try.

There is just too much at risk financially. And, the other reason for improving your culture is this; bringing new talent into a bad environment is the source of a lot of new producer failure. You're just negatively compounding your problem if you don't start with the team you have.

Step #3: Training, Not Just for Skills but Confidence

The two biggest inhibitors to producers taking action and growing their books are apathy and a lack of confidence. You create your best chances to overcome apathy with great goal setting and financial education. To remove the lack of confidence barrier, you must train your producers. Teach your producers the skills they need to Prospect, Sell and Retain. Proper training ensures competence -- an ability to do these tasks successfully. And, from competence comes confidence.

Confidence is a self-fulfilling prophecy, as those without it will often fail (or not try) because they lack it. And those with it succeed, because they have it, make the effort and keep trying.

The Breakdown

Agency Owners come in a lot of different flavors. Many are self-made. They pulled their boots on every morning, trudged into the darkness and came out smelling like a rose. They worked hard and in the face of adversity, they kept putting one foot in front of the other. And when they look back 20 years later, they take pride in the fact they've built one heck of an agency.

If that's you, then you probably never considered the impact of feeling confident -- it wasn't really a choice. You just did what you did and you did it well, and your proof is in the pudding. You have nice cars, a nice house, a beach or mountain home, incredible vacations and a significant net-worth to prove it.

To some degree, you don't really understand those who don't have the confidence, the belief in themselves, like you do.

And you get frustrated, really frustrated. From your perspective, everything they need is out there... it's theirs for the taking. Just go get it; just do what you did.

News Flash! The average person is not like you.

Your brain works faster. If this were basketball instead of selling, it would be obvious to everyone. You hustle. You can see the whole court, and innately, know where your teammates are going. You were blessed, and you can't take enormous credit for it. It's just something you were born with – be grateful. What you can take credit for, is that you continued to develop it on your own.

Let me repeat that. You DEVELOPED it on your own.

But the average person does not have your innate capability. Neither do they have your innate drive. As a general rule, they will not develop it on their own. If the ENVIRONMENT DOES NOT PUSH them, develop them, they will drive in 3rd gear, rather than 5th gear. They will get by, but they won't accelerate to their capability or above their competition.

And like it or not, you have a room full of average people for the most part.

A Message To You:

YOU are the different one. They are the average ones. So, it's up to you to assist them in growing their confidence. And it starts with training, just like in every sport.

It's not their fault they weren't born with that extraordinary inner drive, that sixth sense, that special capability, like you were. You were born with a gift, and you must use it wisely, especially if you want to see your firm experience extraordinary organic growth.

Remember, you don't have a producer problem, you have a leadership problem.

You Have an Innate Ability; Most of Your Producers Don't.

When you're in a stressful selling situation, you have the innate ability to find your way through it and come out a victor. Because you can do that, you think everyone else can too, right?

And that is your problem. The fact that you think everyone else can do it too. But, they can't. Accept that. They need a system, a way of doing things, something they can use to train and build their confidence.

Do a quick test to see if this is true.

Pull your producers in, one at a time, and ask them to lay out their selling process, step-by-step in detail. Will they be able to do it?

The answer you'll get from most of your producers is: *"It just depends."*

Ask an NFL quarterback: *"Where are you going to throw the ball when under pressure"?* They'll tell you exactly how they will read the defense then run through a list in their head, check, check, check, throw. Yes, it depends, but they can tell you what it depends on. They know their playbook and they've watched enough film to know their competition.

As a golfer, when you are 155 yards out, which club are you going to use? They will say *"It depends"*, then they'll tell you exactly what their decision making process is based upon; pin placement, the wind, bunkers and current lie.

Of course, they are professional athletes, they have coaches, they have playbooks; they consistently train to get better.

Aren't your producers professional sales people?

Of course they are, but they don't have a playbook, they don't have practice sessions, they don't study their competition and no one is leading them to do it.

That's why when they say: *"It just depends'*, they don't really mean it. If they were to be totally honest, they'd have to say that they wing it for the most part, that they rely on experience. And that is good... Maybe the golfer shouldn't rely on the caddie to know the distance to flag, the slope of the green, the direction of the wind... They should just wing it. And the NFL quarterback, why not do the same... throw it when it feels right.

You may think that selling is more complex than making your living playing golf or being an NFL quarterback? If so, no need to argue. Just imagine you're standing in the pocket, you have a football in your hand, there are about 4-5 guys that weigh over 300 pounds trying to push your linemen to the side so they can have a clean shot at burying you. At the same time, there are 3-5 receivers zig-zagging across the field while, that many defenders are watching your eyes to see if you will telegraph where you are going to throw the ball so they can intercept it. There are 11 guys on the field just hoping to find a way to embarrass you.

Is selling to one buyer more complex than that? Maybe.

The Root of the Problem

Until you come up with THE way, a process you believe in, you'll never be able to TRAIN them.

And if you don't train them, you'll never move the average person to above average. You'll never help them improve enough to develop a superior level of confidence because every response will be *"It just depends."*

Without the confidence that they can set new business appointments with relative ease, know how to engage a new prospect, build rapport, find pain, get commitment and close the AOR/BOR... you'll never build the sales team of the future.

Without the confidence that they know how to develop a written service plan with their clients, get it in writing, and be able to follow through... they will be stuck at average.

Where does that confidence come from? It comes from training. Where does the training come from - it comes from having a process.

No process, no training, no confidence.

Step #4: Convert That Training and Confidence Into High Leverage Activity - Winning New Business and Booking the Revenue

Before going on that new prospect call, the producer should engage in a Pre-call strategy, with a small team, and **plan** how to win the account.

The hardest part of winning the account is having a very well-defined differentiation strategy. Without differentiation, there's no real need for the prospect to consider a change. And the 'real differentiation' will come from the Proactive Services -- not price and coverage.

Once the Pre-call strategy session is complete, the producer should have a much better opportunity to distinguish and differentiate himself. Compare this to just 'winging it'.

The next step on the Flight Plan is to meet with the prospect, face to face. In that sales call, the process is simple… build rapport, find pain and confirm it, co-create a solution and confirm it, get a commitment that they can fire the incumbent and confirm it.

The two hardest parts are finding pain and getting it confirmed and co-creating a solution and getting it confirmed. There are processes for both of those objectives.

A producer, who is well-trained in these processes, can execute with extraordinary effectiveness. A producer, without proper training, will feel lucky to walk out with a chance to quote the insurance. It's like the difference between a well-trained sniper assassin and the seasonal deer-hunter. The assassin doesn't miss -- Ever.

The next piece is to Pre-close and then present the proposal; there is a whole process there that prevents the last minute counter-attack by the incumbent from being effective. If a producer has done the sales call steps, outlined above, the close should be a no-brainer, but it wouldn't be wise to be overconfident or unprepared.

Money Time...

The incumbent DOES NOT want to lose that continuous stream of income, so they will fight back and it won't always be pretty. Just put yourself in their shoes... what would you do?

There is predictable pattern a smart incumbent will follow; it's a counter-attack. You do that, don't you?

If your producer is not prepared and armed to the hilt, with proper ammo and protective gear, there is a good chance they will fight a good fight and get to the very end and then lose the battle.

If your producer has been trained in a process, it gives them the ability to deal with the incumbent's counter-attack; they radically increase their chance to WIN.

The point is, if you do not have a well-defined, documented process that you believe in, you can't train it. If you can't train it, there's a good chance many of your producers are winging it. If they are winging it, there is good chance the results are average at best.

Skills, Competence, Confidence... Like 1, 2, 3

What happens when a producer does 'the right thing'; they build rapport with their prospect, find coverage gaps, market the account and reduce the price, they present it and then get killed by the incumbent?

What impact does all of this have on their confidence?

You wonder why more new producers don't make it, and you wonder why more veterans don't want to go out and pick a fight on a new account?

What's to wonder? SOMEONE sent them to battle, without proper preparation and battle gear.

Here is the most important part of this equation. If they don't feel confident, they will not put themselves in high-pressure, high-impact situations. They'll glide, slide and avoid.

And, without the confidence to jump into the fire of high-pressure, high-impact situations, they will not grow their books of business.

If your agency is not growing by really high single digits or even double digits year after year, you just discovered why. Your #1 asset for organic growth, your production team, has been neutralized.

Convert their Skill into ACTION

My wife and I have done a decent job of training our 4 kids to be polite, make their beds, help do the dishes and get their homework complete. But, if we don't drive that behavior, they will get a little mouthy, they won't make their beds, they won't help in the kitchen and they procrastinate on their homework.

They are people, and like all people, they have to be driven to do the right thing. Your producers are the same. You can train them and build their skills and confidence, but your job is not done. You have to continue to work to convert those skills into high-leverage actions.

And one of the best ways to do it is to dump your "spreadsheet liars' club" sales meeting and try something different.

What is a "spreadsheet liars' club" sales meeting? They start about 3 days in advance, when your administrative assistant sends out a request for producers: "Please update your pipeline spreadsheet and send to me by Thursday, in preparation for our Monday morning sales meeting."

Then your assistant bundles all of those spreadsheets into a master spreadsheet, and gives them to you, the Agency Owner, on Friday afternoon for you to study over the weekend.

On Monday morning, all the producers show up for the Monday Morning Sales Meeting.

After a little chatter about the weekend, the meeting gets rolling, as you ask the first producer on the list to talk about the accounts he's working on.

So he does a quick review of the accounts he has on the list, then the Agency Owner follows up with: *"Have you lined up your carriers?"* *"Yes Sir, I have"* comes the reply. *"How's your relationship with the prospect?"* *"Pretty good I think"*. *"Tell us more about your strategy."* *"Well, I plan to continue meeting with them and build the relationship. I have loss control coming out soon. We're looking over the policies to see if there are any gaps in coverage. I've got a couple of underwriters that are interested. We're just working through it like always"*. Then your follow-up question, *"Need any help?"* *"No Sir, I'm good"*.

Then on to the next one; then the next and the next.

It's called a "liars' club spreadsheet" sales meeting, not because your producers are lying, but because they seldom say anything of significance.

What's the Purpose of a Sales Meeting?

#1: Drive sales by helping a Producer Beat the Incumbent and Win a New Account.

To drive sales, you have to win the account. To win the account you have to get the other guy fired. To get the other guy fired, you have to have something better. If the only things you have that are better are coverage and price, you're subject to getting rolled.

It seems like reviewing accounts listed on the spreadsheets, having producers talk about them, suggesting carriers, asking about the chance to close, all of that should help drive sales. But for the most part, it doesn't. And why is that?

A clever producer can easily slide their way through the interrogation process brought on by the Agency Owner and yet not accomplish anything towards winning the account. It's more of a reporting meeting than a strategy meeting.

The focus is backwards; therefore you should reverse what you are doing.

Instead of talking about how you are going to sell the account and which carrier you'll use, what if you reversed it and challenged the producer to articulate and defend how they are better than the incumbent agent who already controls the account?

When producers are challenged to **defend** how they are better than the incumbent, how this particular account would be better off with them than they would with the incumbent agent, they get strong; it's like resistance weight training.

It's A Different Conversation

Fact: The incumbent has to get fired for you to get hired.

There is a good chance that the incumbent is a reactive services agent, meaning that once they put the account on the books, all they do is respond to needs as they arise. They are probably not a proactive services agent, and if you are - that's what you must exploit.

Said a different way: "If you do the same thing the incumbent does, the prospect doesn't need you, do they?"

So, when you change the intent of the meeting and challenge the producer to define and defend how they are better than the incumbent, rather than why this is a good prospect, you're using your precious time to help them win and that will drive sales.

Now you are converting Sales Skills into Action, which is what this 4th step is all about.

When you put the incumbent in the room (figuratively speaking) -- then challenge your producer to articulate how they are better than that agent, things get very interesting, and productive.

It makes your differentiation come alive. It makes your sales process come alive. The passion, the ego, the pride, the money... it's all out there for the taking. But only for the

BOLD, confident, assured producer, who knows precisely HOW & WHY he's better.

Now, we have a sales meeting. Now we can convert skills and differentiation training, into something very actionable. This is what will rapidly change your culture and turn your investment into real financial results fast.

Back to the Beginning

If you don't have a core philosophy in your agency that you are absolutely committed to — helping every producer double their personal income — none of this will matter.

If your core philosophy doesn't include a deep belief that your best clients deserve a predictable, valuable client experience — then you've got nothing to sell other than fluff.

If you don't see how this kind of culture would attract new producers like bees to honey, because you provide a vibrant sales culture that trains and arms them, with the knowledge and tools to defeat their competition — then all this growth talk isn't really for you…?

If you don't see your agency as a huge money printing machine that, when operating at full-tilt, spits out money for all to share — then you've missed the point.

However, if you SEE the intelligence of what's being discussed here...

And you **do** want to help your producers...

And you **do** want to service your top clients in an extraordinary way...

And you **do** want to attract new producers, who see your vision...

And you **do** want to rapidly increase the profits and value of your agency...

Then you'll want to change your sales meeting format too.

The right training and proper equipment will build warriors – producers that will grow their books one great prospect at a time. And, in turn, your agency will grow like you've only dreamed possible.

#2: Drive Sales By Helping a Producer Get an Appointment with a Large Target Prospect via an Introduction.

The second purpose of a Sales Meeting is to help a Producer get in the door of a Top Prospect: There is no better way than to have a Top Client make a call on their behalf.

Everyone knows that introductions are the very best form of getting in front of someone. But when your happy, satisfied client actually makes the call for you, well, it just doesn't get any better than that.

But there is fear, angst, trepidation. And these culprits stop most producers in their tracks.

See if you agree with this:

Your producer has clients, who know people the producer wants to meet. Your producer could cold call, leave messages, send emails and letters and most would never get the attention of that prospect. However, the client, with one simple call in most cases, can get right through to that person, because they have an existing peer-to-peer relationship.

These Red Hot Introductions can save days, weeks or even months of effort. This kind of introduction will open doors faster than you can imagine.

Your sales meeting should include a section on helping a producer justify why they deserve to make this request. The best way to do it, is to tell them they probably don't actually deserve it. And then, have them defend why they do.

When your producers are forced to defend why they deserve to get a RED HOT Introduction… it too, is like lifting weights. It makes them stronger. When you do this over and over and over again, guess what happens? Your producers gain more confidence because they become more aware of the great work they do, their confidence goes up; their desire to act is triggered. All the training and processes become second nature: It's muscle memory.

Net Result-

They grow, and in turn, your agency grows. It's a Win/Win of the highest degree. It's worth getting excited about.

Quick review;
Step #1: Commit To Growth
Step #2: You need a Playbook
Step #3: You must train in skills to build confidence
Step #4: Turn skills into action by changing your Sales Meeting

What's left? You've done a lot to grow your producers and you're on the path to removing all their excuses for not producing. There is one last thing you must do; you need to finish it off by creating a culture of accountability. Here's how you do it.

Step #5: The 3 C's to Driving a Culture of Accountability

If you are committed to growth, if you have a playbook or game plan for growth, if you train your producers for competence and confidence -- and if you convert their skills into action, using the CRISP Sales Meeting format -- you are 80% there.

Here is the last 20% -- and it's a must. This step is about what you, as a leader, have to do to create a culture of **Accountability**.

But first, a little analogy...

In order to get your driver's license, you not only had to prove you knew how to drive a car; you had to prove you understood the law. You studied the meaning or the difference between a Red, Yellow and Green light. You had to prove you could read a speed limit sign and that you understood what a speed limit was.

It's all part of getting a driver's license. Along the way, you learned there are policemen that monitor such things as running a red light or speeding. They have equipment to help them with speeding cars; a radar gun.

If you are speeding, they pull you over and write you a warning citation or a ticket. If you get a ticket, you have to pay it, or you face even more serious consequences, even resulting in jail time, if it gets bad enough.

The 3 C's of Accountability are all demonstrated in the story above. Let's talk about each one:

#1: Contract or Written Agreement

If there was no written agreement on what constitutes the law, i.e. what's the meaning of running a red light or of speeding, then it would be awfully hard to enforce anything.

The same is true in an agency environment. If there is no written agreement about how much your book has to grow from year to year to keep your job as a full-fledged, highly paid producer, with enormous freedom to come and go… then there is nothing to enforce.

If you want to step it up in this area of your agency, your first step would be to create your written document defining expectations. No written expectations, there is nothing to hold them accountable to.

What might you put in that Producer Agreement? The first thing is simply this; a minimum book growth clause saying that a book must have an average net growth of a minimum of $25,000 or $50,000 annually, every consecutive year to keep your commission rate where it is now, the maximum. Failing that, a 2% reduction in commission, meaning renewal commission paid, will be reduced from the maximum, say 35% to 33%. If you miss it next year, it will decrease from 33% to 31%. This will continue every year until the minimum is hit at 15% on renewals, the same paid to account managers. That is called a claw-back on commission, as you know. And all of your account managers, who are getting paid like real Producers, will soon be on notice that things are changing and they will get paid like account managers if they don't produce new business and grow their books.

They have the option of becoming students of production, by starting to do what they should have been doing all along -- if they were REAL producers. They will **Prospect, Sell and Retain. Or they'll be paid like Account Managers.**

So the first thing you need in place is the **WRITTEN CONTRACT, the first of 3 C's.** Unless it is all written down in black & white, there is no accountability.

If you are going to do this, and it is highly recommended, then produce the document now and let them know this will go into effect one year from now. That gives them a chance to get in on the production game. Then the following year, if they don't meet the criteria, their renewal commission takes the 2% drop.

#2: The Ability to Count.

If the local policeman or highway patrolman did not have a radar gun, it would be difficult to tell how fast someone was going. All they could rely on is their feeling or opinion.

I bet you've tried this argument, I know I have: "But officer, I set my cruise control on 72 miles an hour, so why are you pulling me over?" The officer says: "The radar clocked you at 82 miles an hour... and it doesn't make mistakes. Here's your ticket." Case closed.

When you're measuring existing books of business, or year over year growth, your agency management system can handle that without difficulty.

But when you're talking about new producers, and you have in your agreement the number of calls, appointments and the number of active accounts that should be in process -- that becomes difficult, unless you have a system that captures all of this information and can report on it, easily.

We'll talk more about systems in a moment. But right now, it's important to recognize: **If you can't COUNT and can't**

MEASURE certain activities -- you CAN'T CREATE ACCOUNTABILITY.

It becomes a game of hearsay or opinions. And you already know; it will wear you out. When producers are under pressure to make money to support their families, they will come up with some whopping white lies to protect themselves and keep their jobs.

So you need a system to count; that's the 2nd of 3 C's.

#3: Consequences

None of this tracking is worth a dime, however, if there are no consequences involved.

In the case of a speeding ticket: What if the officer could pull you over and write you a ticket, but you never had to pay it? Yes, it may be annoying, but it wouldn't change behavior. You hear about this happening on college campuses quite frequently.

Like a football star at the University of Texas, with 137 parking violations. The Dean of Athletics had a conference with him to help clear up matters. Conference? Clear up matters?

If they had a policy that on the 3rd violation you miss a game, on the 6th violation you miss the season and on the 9th you're out of school... It's pretty certain athletes would find a better place to park.

You get the point... no consequences, no behavioral change, that's the 3rd of 3C's; consequences.

There are a few reasons you would not want to instill this sort of accountability. They are:

1. You are **afraid** you will lose your good producers. That's a fair concern, but not a reality, unless your highest performing producers are all 'Prima Donnas.' The problem is, you can't build a sales culture around 'Prima Donnas'; they are too selfish. (If you have one that you feel would be in jeopardy when you raise the standards and you feel you want to keep them, just exclude them from everything).

2. If you have a bunch of underperformers, you might want to protect them from being accountable. Some Agency Owners feel bad that they are changing the rules and expecting people who get paid like producers – and act like account managers - to actually have to produce or get a reduction in pay. It's understandable if you feel that way; there are long term relationships in place. One of your solutions is to form a 'protected group' and exempt them from all the 3 C's of

Accountability. And if you want to do that, do it. It's your agency. Let's just hope that when you are 85 years old they aren't your friends anymore, because they will be asking you for financial favors then also. It might be easier to help them get things right now and pay the short-term price than it would to still be helping them then.

Why Do They Get Away With It?

Why do Agency Owners tolerate these lousy, non-productive behaviors from non-ambitious, apathetic, non-producing producers?

You clearly wouldn't put up with this kind of nonsensical behavior from your CFO, COO, Commercial Manager or CSRs.

Non-performing producers get away with it for a couple of different reasons:

- You don't have a system to develop them, so you feel it is unfair to drive them harder.
- You feel sorry for them, so you are willing to leave them in the puddle of crud, as long as they don't start costing you money.
- You don't feel you have the ability to recruit and hire new talent, so you are stuck with what you've got.

- You and your partners are not that ambitious, so in the big picture it doesn't really matter.

Is it time to draw a line in the sand and say: "It's time for a change; this is how it's going to be going forward."?

Times Have Changed

There is only one reason you will do it: You're running a business. And for a business to thrive, not just survive, it needs to grow and change with the times.

As you know, buggy whip manufacturers are gone. The old cell phone manufacturers are gone. Record stores are gone. Camera film manufacturers are gone. And you can't find a pay phone to save your life.

How many of your Agency Owner buddies have gone by the wayside, selling out because they didn't grow or couldn't grow?

If your goal is extinction, then forget about accountability, forget about hiring new producers, and forget about training and building producer confidence. Maybe it's time to jump aboard your boat and take off into the sunset.

But if your ambition is to GROW your agency and DOMINATE your market, here is something that will help you do just that.

Chapter 6

The Growth Solution

The world is full of people who quietly suffer with unfulfilled desires. Many of them are agency owners that want to grow… They just don't have the intestinal fortitude to push it over the edge; they are dreamers, but not doers.

On the other hand, there are those of you who are ambitious, gritty and driven, for whom high growth is not a question of *if*, but *how*.

If you're chomping at the bit, if your leg is shaking, your heart is racing and your palms are sweaty in anticipation of transforming your agency into a high-performance culture, then you're one of them.

As a competitor at heart, you want to be in that group of agency owners that is talking about 'real organic growth' and the slightest idea that someone else figured it out before you did, is maddening to you.

Human Nature Warning - Even For the Rugged Ones

Warning: Human nature is about to raise its ugly and ragged looking head… and if you're not prepared to deal with it, you're busted. You'll quit before you get started.

Here's how it works…There is an angel sitting on one shoulder and the devil on the other.

The angel is telling you this is a good thing for you and your producers: It's your way to get a lot, by giving a lot.

The angel will tell you: "It's the right thing to do to help your producers become more confident, better sales people, make more money and save more money. You're helping them and their families… and they'll appreciate it even if they have a hard time showing it. Go for it."

Then the devil kicks in with a calming and deep voice as he says: "Don't be stupid! Why are you wasting your precious time and hard-earned money on these people? Sure, some are friends, but if they are such good friends, wouldn't they be trying harder? And the rest of them are idiots… If they could sell, they'd be doing it already. It's not your responsibility to hold their hand and guide them every step of the way; you've got better things to do. Why should you have to spend your money to make them better - let them spend their own money. And, what about your partners? Why do you have to do all of the heavy lifting, while they are out playing golf? Be careful, you're about to talk yourself into something you'll regret. You're about to be sold a bill of goods and you're acting just stupid enough to buy into it. Stop, wake up and smell the roses. Take a vacation…that's how you ought to spend your time and money."

If the devil is not enough to stop you in your tracks, all you have to do is talk to a friendly agency competitor about your growth strategy. They'll certainly have a story about how they tried the exact same thing, but couldn't move the needle. They did sales training… changed their sales meetings, invested in a CRM system. Nothing worked, so they went back to the way it was (they quit).

Time to Get Real

A Realist would say: "Let's dig in to the facts, the truth… the reality. Is our growth challenge a producer problem or a leadership problem?"

If it's a producer problem, will it work itself out without intervention? If it's not a producer problem, it must be a leadership problem. And from there s/he will start asking the bold and honest questions;

1. How much potential is embedded in my producer force, so that with training, coaching and systems we can create a win/win situation, meaning <u>more revenue for the firm</u> and <u>more personal income for the producer</u>?

2. Is it my responsibility to fix the problem, or should I just be hopeful that it will get better?

3. Do I already have the skills and ability I need to do this job, and does my past reflect that? Or, do I need to grow my skills and ability in order to accomplish this?

4. When considering the investment in time and money, is it worth it, will it create a significant return?

5. If I do take action, where will it get us in 5 years?

6. If I don't take action, where will we be in 5 years?

7. Of all the things I am responsible for, where does this responsibility rank; Top 5, Top 3 or #1?

The difference between where your agency is today and where it will be 5 years from now is in direct proportion to your ability to <u>develop your sales team.</u>

Think about the gravity of that quote.

If your next 5 years are a repeat of your last 5 years, are you going to be satisfied? If the answer is NO, you have to Act now, don't you?

An exercise that you'd probably rather avoid, is listing out your producers, one by one, with age, new business written, and book size. Then project where each of those people will be 5 years from now, based upon their current and past performance. One thing is sure; they'll all be 5 years older. How many of them will have a book twice the size or even 50% larger than it is now? How many will even grow enough to beat inflation rates, if you don't drive it?

When you do this, the next and most important step, is to calculate and project the potential or the pent-up opportunity, but undeveloped capability, in your producers. This is another brutal reality test. If indeed your producers are doing all they can do, they are tapped out, living up to their potential, they are near maxed-out, then your future is very predictable; bleak but predictable.

If there is potential, then it's up to you, the leader – not them, to create an environment with systems, processes and training to develop it. The burden is on your shoulders, not theirs.

You have to make a decision. <u>Will you develop it or let it rot on the vine?</u> Will you train it, coach it up, make them better, or leave them on their own?

If you find yourself saying something like: "What if they don't want to cooperate? What if they aren't interested in growing? What if they are content and satisfied with their income? What if they are old and incapable?" What do I do then?

Being a Realist, you already know you will have uncooperative types. You will have those that are not interested in growing. You will have those that are satisfied and content; it's to be expected.

But who cares? That's why they need a SALES LEADER not a follower. Someone that will stimulate, agitate and promulgate rapid change and growth.

Void of Leaders

Most independent insurance agencies are void of sales leaders. They are run by either a self-indulged producer, focused on building his own book, or an underwriter trying to eliminate any risk in his agency. There are very few Sales Leaders and that's why the opportunity is enormous for anyone that wants to step up to the plate.

Look, to be the leader you are capable of being, you have to get over the fact that your producers aren't asking you for help or assistance. In fact, they will probably resist it.

- They will never ask you to be more demanding of them.

- They'll never ask you to hold them accountable.

- They will never ask you to train them.

- They'll never ask you to run them through in-depth goal setting.

But, please don't be foolish - they need it and they need it badly.

And whoever is bold enough, driven enough, competitive enough to pick up the torch and go do it, will win the race.

Is that you?

If it is you, your next step is fairly simple.

Let's start by reviewing The 5 Steps to Extraordinary Growth that were laid out in Chapter 5.

Here is a quick summary:

Step #1: Adopt a 'Winners never Quit' Commitment to Growth - the only reason an agency isn't growing rapidly is they never committed. They might have tried, but didn't stick with it, they quit. That's at a corporate level. There are 2 other commitments:

1. Commit to being a proactive services firm – provide a unique and differentiated client experience; this gives your producers something concrete to sell.

2. Commit to your producers – help your producers double their personal income in 3-5 years with ½ the accounts.

Step #2: To do this, you need a playbook, a business process - a proven path for opening doors, winning accounts and keeping them for a lifetime. The Flight Plan as described in Chapter 5 provides a high level overview.

Step #3: Training, not just for skills and to improve their effectiveness, but to instill confidence in your producers. (This is where most agencies sorely drop the ball. No one gets better without training. Look at athletes, musicians, actors and now salespeople.)

Step #4: Convert that training and confidence into money – into getting into bigger prospects and taking that business from the competitor by running great sales meetings. (Dump the "spreadsheet liars' club" sales meetings, and the town hall meetings and the book of the month club. Help your producers open doors and win business with CRISP (Continuous and Rapid Improvement Sales Process) Sales Meetings.

Step #5: Create a No-Excuses Culture of Accountability

1. Create a written agreement with each producer - spell out exactly what you expect of each other.

2. Implement cutting-edge technology to help you count and measure activities and pipelines. (If you can't count, you can't have accountability)

3. Set consequences, for both positive and negative behaviors: If they sell and grow, reward them. If they sit on their book, don't prospect, don't sell and don't write new business… then pay them like an account manager, not a producer.

Upgrade Your Hiring Process

If you're hitting on all cylinders with your hiring of newbies, then stick with it. If not, you need to upgrade your hiring process. This is PARAMOUNT.

When you can determine, up-front, with a high degree of accuracy if a candidate can and will make it as a producer, you've changed your agency forever.

Stop giving mediocre candidates a shot at being a producer. When you implement this process, you'll make good hires. When you make good hires and put them in the environment laid out in the 5 Steps to Extraordinary Growth, you are virtually guaranteed to be more successful. If you hire great talent and put them in a non-productive environment, survival rates go way down. And what's horrible, is they will get picked up by a 'better' agency, with a better sales culture and probably do well… mostly at your expense.

There are specific things you need to do to qualify a new producer.

Here is a quick review of the 6 MUST-HAVE characteristics EVERY new producer should bring to the table and, if not... **Do. Not. Hire. Them.**

1. The ability to deal with rejection - if they don't have this, they won't prospect. If they don't prospect, they will have no one to sell to and are guaranteed to fail.

2. They have to be street and book smart - if they are not, they won't figure out how to get past the gatekeeper, they won't figure out how to get the quote they need from the underwriter and they won't figure out how to out-fox the incumbent.

3. Driven - if they are not driven, then once they make enough money to buy a boat, they will quit growing their book of business.

4. Great at relationships - people like to do business with people they like.

5. Resilient - if they are not resilient, gritty, they will quit when the going gets tough. It will get tough; it's guaranteed.

6. Coachable - or they won't learn from their mistakes.

As I mentioned before, there is a way to determine if a producer will make it before you hire them and I've given you the overview.

My new book *GRIT: Find, Hire, Develop Producers That Are Motivated To Prospect & Sell* will fill in the holes for you and coach you through the process that our top clients use.

Does it work? Here is one brief case study.

From 1995 to 2005, the firm Higginbotham hired 34 producers and retained 29 of them. Executives located the candidates and Randy vetted them.

Higginbotham's revenue grew from $4 million to $30 million during that decade, and those 29 newly hired producers grew their personal books of business to a combined $17.5 million.

The firm's organic growth has averaged in the double digits over a 20-year period.

For a quick summary of the hiring process go here:

http://www.thewedge.net/newproducerguide

Time is Money and Speed is Imperative.

If you want a paint-by-the-numbers, easy to implement, step-by-step process to grow your agency, this is what I've got for you…

Since March of 1992, I've been in a constant development phase with the goal to build the most effective system that will solve agency owner's problems… it's called the iWin Agency Growth System.

The Problems the iWin Agency Growth System Solves:

1. Unmotivated producers; lacking focus and direction.
2. Poor time utilization; avoiding high leverage money generating activities.
3. Poorly defined differentiation; making it difficult to stand out in a crowded buyer's market.
4. Empty pipelines; not enough new business appointments being set.
5. Weak sales strategy; inability to find or create buyer's pain.
6. Not getting deal closed; Incumbent Agent getting Last-look and keeping the business.
7. Account retention; too much time having to defend renewal.

8. Missed cross-sell opportunities; poor planning, lack of trust or respect amongst team.

If you have trouble getting your producers to:

- Leverage your value-added differences
- Write larger accounts

If you've struggled with:

- Running great sales meetings
- Creating producer confidence
- Finding, hiring and developing new producers

Then you absolutely owe it to yourself to research and investigate the best way to close the gap between potential and performance.

The *iWin Agency Growth System* was designed from the ground up to help Sales Leaders turn an average firm into an Agency Growth Machine.

To do so takes effort, but it's not Superman effort. It's not heroic effort… it's a consistent implementation of solid principles and basic activities that makes sense to any rational business person.

So if you are serious about growth, I want to help you save a lot of time, and create a massive short-cut to growing your agency.

Our clients will tell you that the *iWin Agency Growth System* is the most comprehensive All-in-One Growth SYSTEM ever built for commercial insurance agencies, and more importantly, it works.

With **The iWin Agency Growth System,** you can build a **team of High Performing Producers, an Organic Growth Agency.**

The *iWin Agency Growth System* gives agency owners and sales leaders **everything** they need for growth… all in ONE place.

You'll get the **best in class, right at your fingertips:**

- Sales training
- Sales meetings
- New producer hiring and onboarding process
- Pipeline management tools
- Executive coaching and support

Here is our PROMISE; you won't find anything as comprehensive, complete and effective to enable you to grow your agency.

Your Next Step

If you want a short-cut, saving hundreds of hours and a lot of developmental dollars, to help you overcome;

- Unmotivated producers
- Selling on Price
- Getting rolled by the incumbent
- Missing their sales goals year after year

And you want to end the struggle of finding, hiring and developing new producers, you'll find your solution right here: http://www.thewedge.net

Take a Tour

Take **a self-guided tour** of the *iWin Agency Growth System*: You'll see the incredible tools and processes that have been built for you to grow your agency, with speed and efficiency… short-cuts everywhere you turn.

http://thewedge.net/indepth/

Agency Growth

It's not rocket science. But it's definitely not kindergarten either. If you want to turn on your Agency Growth Machine, visit us at...

http://www.thewedge.net

References

Reagan Consulting. 2009. *Producer Recruiting & Development: Getting the Attention It Deserves-Achieving the Results You Need.*

Cherry, Kendra. *What is Intrinsic Motivation.* Retrieved November 20, 2015 from http://psychology.about.com

"Pipedream" [Def. 1]. *Oxford Dictionary of English,* 3rd Edition. 2010. Print

Marsh Berry. *Average Agencies vs. High Growth Agencies Graphs*

About the Author
Randy Schwantz

Mission: Help Agency Owners develop rapidly growing firms and help Producers DOUBLE their personal income by gaining and retaining new clients.

Randy began in 1992 to change the way insurance was sold, with a unique process that stopped producers from getting rolled by the incumbent at the end of the sales process ... this powerful process is called The Wedge.

Today, **Randy and his staff actively Coach 93 agencies with 783 producers controlling over a Billion dollars of agency revenue, and that number is rapidly growing.** He has established one the largest and fastest growing sales consulting firms in the world for insurance agencies.

He learned in the trenches, having conducted over 2,500 sales meetings, thousands of one-on-one coaching sessions with producers, and training over 5,200 producers in The Wedge sales process... totaling over **22,000 hours face to face** with insurance producers and sales leaders.

He has a tenacious drive to succeed **and passion to help others.**

Randy is married to his wife of 27 years, Lori and together they have 4 daughters. His mission to help Producers Double their

About the Author Randy Schwantz

Personal Income is driven from his own personal experience. You will hear him say "Raising four daughters is pretty expensive when you consider the cost of 4 cars, 4 universities and 4 weddings, not to mention funding our own retirement".

He often reminds producers, **"It's not just how much you make, it's how much you save that provides financial freedom."**

Astute Producers have the ability to become powerful and wealthy when they plan and execute on a strategy to Double Their Personal Income…and Randy's mission is to help them achieve it!

Author of 7 insightful, life-and-income-changing books including **The Wedge: How To Stop Selling and Start Winning, GRIT: How To Find, Hire, Develop Elite Producers** and **How To Get Your Competition Fired (without saying anything bad about them).**

He has been interviewed by ABC World News Today, been written about in the New York Times, Entrepreneur Magazine, business journals and internet media all over the world.

As seen on

What Others Are Saying About...

The Book, iWin, and The Wedge

Ten years ago I began using *The Wedge*. I saw personal extraordinary growth in my book of business. Then my agency began to employ the processes and we have never looked back. This book *Agency Growth Machine* lays out exactly what you need to experience a high level of growth within your agency. There's no need for months of strategy meetings or trial and error experimentation. These methods are proven. They work.

Joel Stanley, Senior VP, Sales Training, Assured Neace Lukens, Louisville, KY

This book is not for the faint of heart. Randy forces you, as a leader, to look yourself in the mirror and determine if you are man (or in my case woman) enough to revolutionize your sales culture. A must read if you are looking for a way to crawl out from the marginal growth trap and really nail it!

Laura Deeley Bren, Atlantic/Smith, Cropper & Deeley, Willards, MD

After 27 years as an independent agent, everything changed for me when I met Randy Schwantz and signed on as an *iWin Agency Growth System* agent four years ago. Since then, business is much more profitable and much more fun. Everything he taught me is in this book and it all works.

John Marchetti, MRB, Ridgeland, MS

Building on The Wedge, *Agency Growth Machine* provides clear concise strategies for any CEO seeking to re-energize a flat line sales environment. After 35 years in sales and getting rolled countless times, this book proves old dogs can learn new tricks, while helping launch any sales team with renewed confidence.

Jim DeVolld, LP Insurance, Reno, NV

As an agency owner, you find yourself pulled in a number of different directions which makes it difficult to focus on what matters most – developing effective sales people. Randy's book, The *Agency Growth Machine*, provides a blueprint, which outlines specific steps and processes to help agency owners build an effective sales organization and culture.

Bill Holman, Holman Insurance, Atlanta, GA

Several years ago we made a decision to differentiate our agency by offering proactive services that focus on workers compensation. We hired high level employees, purchased the latest software, started a marketing campaign, offered all kinds of great services, but we still struggled to increase sales. It wasn't until working with Randy and *The Wedge* that we finally figured out how to take what makes us different and convert that into new sales. Randy has changed our culture. Our new business, referrals, closing ratios, BORs, and account sizes are the highest they've ever been. Randy's method has us focused on the factors that determine success, selling commercial insurance. It works!

Jason L. Ressler, Teeter Group, Altoona, PA

15 years ago, InterWest decided it needed to begin reinvesting, to a significant degree, in the next generation of producers; a very costly venture, if not done correctly. The old method of hiring and development with a 70% failure rate was not an option; we needed something different. We brought Randy and his philosophy into our organization and continue a close relationship to this day; why? Randy helped in defining our sales culture and refining our hiring process. Randy made it clear from the very start that formal training is easy - ongoing implementation is the difficult part. *The Wedge* process brought something that every producer - new and old - could use, and more importantly it brought a sales language that our entire staff has been able to embrace. The results speak for themselves: 70% of our new producer hires succeed rather than fail, accountability and peer support comes through CRISP meetings, closing ratios on new business exceed 50%; the list goes on. All of this has lead to solid double digit organic growth turning a massive reinvestment into significant top and bottom line growth.
Keith Schuler, Interwest Insurance Services, Sacramento, CA

If you don't want new producers hitting the ground running and producing revenue in their first 60 days, then don't introduce them to *The Wedge*! The myth, that it takes a new producer a year to learn insurance before they can produce revenue, is garbage; learn *The Wedge* and get the incumbent fired! It works!
Louis Berman, Neace Lukens, Charleston, SC

If you don't grow, you plateau: You don't have a solid foundation to perpetuate and the only alternative is to sell. The largest universal missing piece to agency perpetuation plans is, they don't have the horses, the people, to make it happen. The *Agency Growth Machine* provides a blueprint to make it happen; to develop the dynamic sales team to grow the agency and to be the foundation to perpetuate.

Tim Cunningham. OPTIS Partners, LLC, Chicago, Illinois

Randy Schwantz helped transform the way we think about sales. Before, producers in our firm were happy to quote. *The Wedge* transformed our thinking. As a firm we've become much more strategic in our thinking. Now our focus is on winning!

Rusty Reid, Higginbotham, Fort Worth, TX

We use everything Randy talks about in this book. Since implementing the *iWin Agency Growth System*, our agency has consistently met or exceeded our new business goals. Randy's sales process forces us to differentiate ourselves from competitors and we routinely win new accounts by BOR. Implementing this sales process is the best thing you can do to improve results at your agency.

Joe Padula, GenCorp, East Greenwich, RI

Randy's insight into the discipline of the insurance sales process is on target in his new book *Agency Growth Machine*. He has spent a career perfecting his sales system *The Wedge* and the *iWin Agency Growth System*. It has proven to be effective for agencies of all sizes. The BroadStreet Core Partner agencies who embrace his system and develop its sales techniques, continually outperform the industry in organic sales and producer development.

Rick Miley, Broadstreet Partners, Columbus, OH

For as long as I have been an insurance agency leader I have known that sustainable growth is the difference between success and failure. During my stretch at a large public firm the expensive and ineffective process of hiring multiple new producers, and by chance keeping the few average and rare exceptional producers, was standard practice (Otherwise known as 'seeing what sticks'). Since becoming an owner of a smaller agency, the scale required to make 'seeing what sticks' work is not practical. Frankly it was not practical at a large firm either, just easier to hide poor results. We clearly needed a process that could help us weed out the resource suckers and focus on winners.

The widespread quick fix, paint by numbers, solutions were alluring, but like anything that is too good to be true - they were. What Randy offers is by no means that. This is a workable plan, that with unwavering commitment and elbow grease we can hire, train and inspire new and existing producers to achieve million dollar results.

Bob Iocco, Trustpoint Insurance, Bristol, VA

The best thing about Randy's system is that it is self-reinforcing, highly effective and there's integrity in it. Your approach aligns with human nature, the psychology of decision-making, and works with what's best in us, not against. There's no slick bullshit, no selling ice to Eskimos, no always be closing, etc. Over the past 15 years, I found that the more intelligent and successful the sales professional, the more they understand and integrate Randy's approach: *The Wedge*.

Ken Ewell, The Graham Company, Philadelphia, PA

What Others Are Saying About...

The Book, iWin, and The Wedge

Creating a strong sales culture is ultimately the most important, but also the most challenging thing your organization can accomplish. The materials from Randy and the *iWin Agency Growth System* are a quintessential resource for achieving that task. Randy hits on all the essential elements for executing your sales culture: Hiring, Training, Motivating, Differentiation and Accountability. I've used his materials for 15+ years… they work.
Stephen Geoffray, First United Insurance Solutions, McKinney, TX

The importance of achieving organic growth for our firm is paramount to our continued success. We place strong emphasis on producer hiring, producer accountability, improved retention ratios and cross selling techniques to improve our sales efforts. We utilize the *Wedge Sales process* in concert with the *iWin* product and the results have been outstanding. We think of Randy as our outsourced coach and partner in improving our sales results. What a great partner.
Steve Deal, Assured Partners, Lake Mary, FL

You really have only two paths to growing your agency: Playing the miserable game of assigning markets and quoting, or getting the incumbent fired. It's that simple. The *Agency Growth Machine*, properly executed, will show you how to win."
Michael Der Manouel, Jr. , Der Manouel Insurance, Fresno, CA

Lloyd Sadd has been practicing the principles of *The Wedge* and working with Randy Schwantz for over 15 years! We will not allow new employees to meet with prospective clients until they are *Wedge* trained! *The Wedge* is our foundation to organic growth and has helped us take our firm from $2.5 million in revenue to over $30 million in revenue in fifteen years.
T. Marshall Sadd, Lloyd Sadd Insurance Brokers, Canada

164

What Others Are Saying About...

The Book, iWin, and The Wedge

Bill Walsh changed professional football with his west coast offense. Randy Schwantz is the Bill Walsh of the insurance industry and has changed the game. We all want the playbook of the winning team. The *Agency Growth Machine* is the playbook that will make your agency a winning team. As for me personally, *The Wedge* changed the way I was doing business. I understood some of the concepts that Randy taught in *The Wedge* but did not have a formal system. *The Wedge* gave me a system and helped me sell more business with less effort. I practice quote 0% now and write most of my business on broker of record.

Mike Dennis, Conrad Houston, Anchorage, AK

Read the book; it is a great review of the successful process. Then call Randy and make a commitment to move your agency to the upper tier of performance and value.

Jim Henderson, Assured Partners, Lake Mary, FL

Randy has the answers to the key issues faced by all sales managers and agency principals: How do I get close to 100% of my new producer hires to succeed and how do I get 80% of my producers driving our firm aggressively forward? Randy's most insightful and game changing book since *The Wedge*!

Liz Bishop, Heffernan Insurance, Walnut Creek, CA

Randy helped us develop a sales culture that drives consistent 15-20% growth year to year. We hire good people, and Randy's system makes them Million Dollar Producers.

Mike Shanahan, HM Risk, St. Louis, MO

What Others Are Saying About...

The Book, iWin, and The Wedge

Excuse time is over! In his latest book, *The Agency Growth Machine*, Randy Schwantz captures all critical elements for producing genuine organic growth within an insurance agency. If you are an agency owner who really wants to create a legacy with your agency, rather than cash out, read the book now. I've owned my own agency for over 15 years. Over this time period, I searched high and low for a comprehensive selling system designed specifically for our industry and found none until I found Schwantz's *iWin Agency Growth System*. Now, Schwantz raises the bar once again with a guide that provides an overview of the entire system. It shows the big picture. It demonstrates how to produce results for your firm. It removes the excuses that we have become so accustomed to making in our industry.

Dirk Fournier, Fournier Group, Portland, OR

As a new producer, I was fortunate to meet Randy about 17 years ago and learn The Wedge. In our firm, we have deployed everything he talks about in his new book, *Agency Growth Machine*. Our producers have benefited greatly and our firm has seen tremendous growth. Randy and his system are truly the only ones proven within our industry from my perspective. Thank you Randy for what you have helped us accomplish and what I hope we continue to accomplish in the future.

Lee Rogers, Rogers Insurance Ltd., Calgary, AB, Canada

By following Randy's Agency Growth System my producers are more focused on winning business and writing larger accounts. As a sales manager, Randy's line: "This is how it is going to be going forward" really hit home for me. Sales managers have to be consistent and push their producers. I highly recommend Randy's system if you want to grow, train and hold producers accountable.

Patrick Darcey, Provider Group, Needham, MA

What Others Are Saying About...

The Book, iWin, and The Wedge

We've been using *The Wedge* and the *iWin Agency Growth System* for almost a year now, and it's been an excellent fit for our agency. As a young owner of a firm, that already does some proactive service, it has helped us establish a track to run on, with the goal toward writing more business via BOR, and helping our own clients better reach their goals. I would highly recommend Randy and his team for anyone interested in becoming more than just a vendor to their current client base.

Josh Kilmer, The Kilmer Group, Wyalusing, PA

Prior to adopting Randy's *iWin Agency Growth System*, we were 'business as usual', including making presentations based solely on coverage and price. After attending Randy's training, we realized the *iWin Agency Growth System* is much more than The Wedge training. Over the past 20 months, we have re-evaluated the way we approach new business clients, run sales meetings, hired new producers as well as establishing proactive service standards for our existing clients. The *iWin* program has had an immensely positive and profound effect on our organization.

Glenn D. Burcham, Arthur Hall Insurance, West Chester, PA

The Wedge has become an integral part of our sales process and in everything we do with new business development and client retention. Now, the *iWin Agency Growth System* was the missing piece in adopting a process to become a true sales organization. With Randy's guidance, we have revamped our entire process of pre-call strategies, red hot introductions and now conducting meaningful and result driven sales meetings; quite a difference as our agency culture has improved dramatically.

Michael McDermott, McDermott Costa, San Leandro, CA

What Others Are Saying About...

The Book, iWin, and The Wedge

Several years ago, Randy helped get us started on our growth track. Focusing on over-serving the Top 20% and trading down the bottom 80% has helped us create 14 new Million Dollar Producers. The concepts worked then, and they work now.

Michael Ferreira, Propel, Tacoma, WA

For more inspiration visit us at:

http://thewedge.net/success-stories/

168